TERENCE RATTIGAN

Born in 1911, a scholar at Harrow and at Trinity College, Oxford, Terence Rattigan had his first long-running hit in the West End at the age of twenty-five: *French Without Tears* (1936). His next play, *After the Dance* (1939), opened to euphoric reviews yet closed under the gathering clouds of war, but with *Flare Path* (1942) Rattigan embarked on an almost unbroken series of successes, with most plays running in the West End for at least a year and several making the transition to Broadway: *While the Sun Shines* (1943), *Love in Idleness* (1944), *The Winslow Boy* (1946), *The Browning Version* (performed in double-bill with *Harlequinade*, 1948), *Who is Sylvia?* (1950), *The Deep Blue Sea* (1952), *The Sleeping Prince* (1953) and *Separate Tables* (1954). From the mid-fifties, with the advent of the 'Angry Young Men', he enjoyed less success on stage, though *Ross* (1960) and *In Praise of Love* (1973) were well received. As well as seeing many of his plays turned into successful films, Rattigan wrote a number of original plays for television from the fifties onwards. He was knighted in 1971 and died in 1977.

D1638266

**Other titles by the same author
published by Nick Hern Books**

After the Dance

The Browning Version and *Harlequinade*

The Deep Blue Sea

First Episode

Flare Path

French Without Tears

In Praise of Love

Love in Idleness

Rattigan's Nijinsky
(adapted from Rattigan's screenplay by Nicholas Wright)

Separate Tables

Who is Sylvia? and *Duologue*

The Winslow Boy

Terence Rattigan

CAUSE CÉLÈBRE

Introduced by
Dan Rebellato

NICK HERN BOOKS

London

www.nickhernbooks.co.uk

A Nick Hern Book

This edition of *Cause Célèbre* first published in Great Britain in 2011 as a paperback original by Nick Hern Books Limited, 14 Larden Road, London W3 7ST. *Cause Célèbre* was first published in 1978 by Hamish Hamilton Limited

Copyright © 1978 Trustees of the Terence Rattigan Trust
Introduction copyright © 2011 Dan Rebellato

Front cover photo copyright © Hulton Deutsch Collection
Cover design by Ned Hoste, 2H

Typeset by Nick Hern Books, London
Printed in the UK by CLE Print Ltd, St Ives, Cambs, PE27 3LE

A CIP catalogue record for this book is available from the British Library

ISBN 978 1 85459 207 1

FSC
www.fsc.org
MIX
From responsible
sources
FSC® C019549

Terence Rattigan (1911–1977)

Terence Rattigan stood on the steps of the Royal Court Theatre, on 8 May 1956, after the opening night of John Osborne's *Look Back in Anger*. Asked by a reporter what he thought of the play, he replied, with an uncharacteristic lack of discretion, that it should have been retitled 'Look how unlike Terence Rattigan I'm being.'[1] And he was right. The great shifts in British theatre, marked by Osborne's famous premiere, ushered in kinds of playwriting which were specifically unlike Rattigan's work. The pre-eminence of playwriting as a formal craft, the subtle tracing of the emotional lives of the middle classes – those techniques which Rattigan so perfected – fell dramatically out of favour, creating a veil of prejudice through which his work even now struggles to be seen.

Terence Mervyn Rattigan was born on 10 June 1911, a wet Saturday a few days before George V's coronation. His father, Frank, was in the diplomatic corps and Terry's parents were often posted abroad, leaving him to be raised by his paternal grandmother. Frank Rattigan was a geographically and emotionally distant man, who pursued a string of little-disguised affairs throughout his marriage. Rattigan would later draw on these memories when he created Mark St Neots, the bourgeois Casanova of *Who is Sylvia?* Rattigan was much closer to his mother, Vera Rattigan, and they remained close friends until her death in 1971.

Rattigan's parents were not great theatregoers, but Frank Rattigan's brother had married a Gaiety Girl, causing a minor family uproar, and an apocryphal story suggests that the 'indulgent aunt' reported as taking the young Rattigan to the theatre may have been this scandalous relation.[2] And when, in the summer of 1922, his family went to stay in the country cottage of the drama critic Hubert Griffiths, Rattigan avidly worked through his extensive library of playscripts. Terry went to Harrow in 1925, and there maintained both his somewhat illicit theatregoing habit and his insatiable reading, reputedly devouring every play in the school library. Apart from contemporary authors like Galsworthy, Shaw and Barrie, he also read the plays of Chekhov, a writer whose crucial influence he often acknowledged.[3]

His early attempts at writing, while giving little sign of his later sophistication, do indicate his ability to absorb and reproduce his own theatrical experiences. There was a ten-minute melodrama about the Borgias entitled *The Parchment*, on the cover of which the author recommends with admirable conviction that a suitable cast for this work might comprise 'Godfrey Tearle, Gladys Cooper, Marie Tempest, Matheson Lang, Isobel Elsom, Henry Ainley... [and] Noël Coward'.[4] At Harrow, when one of his teachers demanded a French playlet for a composition exercise, Rattigan, undaunted by his linguistic shortcomings, produced a full-throated tragedy of deception, passion and revenge which included the immortal curtain line: 'COMTESSE. (*Souffrant terriblement.*) Non! non! non! Ah non! Mon Dieu, non!'[5] His teacher's now famous response was 'French execrable: theatre sense first class'.[6] A year later, aged fifteen, he wrote *The Pure in Heart,* a rather more substantial play showing a family being pulled apart by a son's crime and the father's desire to maintain his reputation. Rattigan's ambitions were plainly indicated on the title pages, each of which announced the author to be 'the famous playwrite and author T. M. Rattigan.'[7]

Frank Rattigan was less than keen on having a 'playwrite' for a son and was greatly relieved when in 1930, paving the way for a life as a diplomat, Rattigan gained a scholarship to read History at Trinity, Oxford. But Rattigan's interests were entirely elsewhere. A burgeoning political conscience that had led him to oppose the compulsory Officer Training Corps parades at Harrow saw him voice pacifist and socialist arguments at college, even supporting the controversial Oxford Union motion 'This House will in no circumstances fight for its King and Country' in February 1933. The rise of Hitler (which he briefly saw close at hand when he spent some weeks in the Black Forest in July 1933) and the outbreak of the Spanish Civil War saw his radical leanings deepen and intensify. Rattigan never lost his political compassion. After the war he drifted towards the Liberal Party, but he always insisted that he had never voted Conservative, despite the later conception of him as a Tory playwright of the establishment.[8]

Away from the troubled atmosphere of his family, Rattigan began to gain in confidence as the contours of his ambitions and his identity moved more sharply into focus. He soon took advantage of the university's theatrical facilities and traditions. He joined the Oxford Union Dramatic Society (OUDS), where contemporaries included Giles Playfair, George Devine, Peter Glenville, Angus Wilson and Frith Banbury. Each year, OUDS ran a one-act play competition and in Autumn 1931 Rattigan submitted one. Unusually, it seems that this was a highly experimental effort, somewhat like Konstantin's piece in *The Seagull*. George Devine, the OUDS president, apparently told the young author, 'Some of it is absolutely smashing, but it goes too far.'[9] Rattigan was instead to make his first mark as a somewhat scornful reviewer for the student newspaper, *Cherwell*, and as a performer in the Smokers (OUDS's private revue club), where he adopted the persona and dress of 'Lady Diana Coutigan', a drag performance which allowed him to discuss leading members of the Society with a barbed camp wit.[10]

That the name of his Smokers persona echoed the contemporary phrase, 'queer as a coot', indicates Rattigan's new-found confidence in his homosexuality. In February 1932, Rattigan played a tiny part in the OUDS production of *Romeo and Juliet*, which was directed by John Gielgud and starred Peggy Ashcroft and Edith Evans (women undergraduates were not admitted to OUDS, and professional actresses were often recruited). Rattigan's failure to deliver his one line correctly raised an increasingly embarrassing laugh every night (an episode which he reuses to great effect in *Harlequinade*). However, out of this production came a friendship with Gielgud and his partner, John Perry. Through them, Rattigan was introduced to theatrical and homosexual circles, where his youthful 'school captain' looks were much admired.

A growing confidence in his sexuality and in his writing led to his first major play. In 1931, he shared rooms with a contemporary of his, Philip Heimann, who was having an affair with Irina Basilevich, a mature student. Rattigan's own feelings for Heimann completed an eternal triangle that formed the basis of the play he co-wrote with Heimann, *First Episode*. This play was accepted for production in Surrey's 'Q' theatre; it was respectfully received and subsequently transferred to the Comedy Theatre in London's West End, though carefully shorn of its homosexual subplot. Despite receiving only £50 from this production (and having put £200 into it), Rattigan immediately dropped out of college to become a full-time writer.

Frank Rattigan was displeased by this move, but made a deal with his son. He would give him an allowance of £200 a year for two years and let him live at home to write; if at the end of that period, he had had no discernible success, he would enter a more secure and respectable profession. With this looming deadline, Rattigan wrote quickly. *Black Forest*, an O'Neill-inspired play based on his experiences in Germany in 1933, is one of the three that have survived. Rather unwillingly, he collaborated with Hector Bolitho on an adaptation of the latter's novel, *Grey Farm*, which received a disastrous New York production in 1940. Another project was an adaptation of *A Tale of Two Cities*, written with Gielgud; this fell through at the last minute when Donald Albery, the play's potential producer, received a complaint from actor-manager John Martin-Harvey who was beginning a farewell tour of his own adaptation, *The Only Way*, which he had been performing for forty-five years. As minor compensation, Albery invited Rattigan to send him any other new scripts. Rattigan sent him a play provisionally titled *Gone Away*, based on his experiences in a French-language summer school in 1931. Albery took out a nine-month option on it, but no production appeared.

By mid-1936, Rattigan was despairing. His father had secured him a job with Warner Brothers as an in-house screenwriter, which was reasonably paid; but Rattigan wanted success in the theatre, and his desk-bound life at Teddington Studios seemed unlikely to advance this ambition. By chance, one of Albery's productions was unexpectedly losing money, and the wisest course of action seemed to be to pull the show and replace it with something cheap. Since *Gone Away* required a relatively small cast and only one set, Albery quickly arranged for a production. Harold French, the play's director, had only one qualm: the title. Rattigan suggested *French Without Tears*, which was immediately adopted.

After an appalling dress rehearsal, no one anticipated the rapturous response of the first-night audience, led by Cicely Courtneidge's infectious laugh. The following morning Kay Hammond, the show's female lead, discovered Rattigan surrounded by the next day's reviews. 'But I don't believe it,' he said. 'Even *The Times* likes it.'[11]

French Without Tears played over 1000 performances in its three-year run and Rattigan was soon earning £100 a week. He moved out of his father's home, wriggled out of his Warner Brothers contract, and dedicated himself to spending the money as soon as it came in. Partly this was an attempt to defer the moment when he had to follow up this enormous success. In the event, both of his next plays were undermined by the outbreak of war.

After the Dance, an altogether more bleak indictment of the Bright Young Things' failure to engage with the iniquities and miseries of contemporary life, opened, in June 1939, to euphoric reviews; but only a month later the European crisis was darkening the national mood and audiences began to dwindle. The play was pulled in August after only sixty performances. *Follow My Leader* was a satirical farce closely based on the rise of Hitler, co-written with an Oxford contemporary, Tony Goldschmidt (writing as Anthony Maurice in case anyone thought he was German). It suffered an alternative fate. Banned from production in 1938, owing to the Foreign Office's belief that 'the production of this play at this time would not be in the best interests of the country',[12] it finally received its premiere in 1940, by which time Rattigan and Goldschmidt's mild satire failed to capture the real fears that the war was unleashing in the country.

Rattigan's insecurity about writing now deepened. An interest in Freud, dating back to his Harrow days, encouraged him to visit a psychiatrist that he had known while at Oxford, Dr Keith Newman. Newman exerted a Svengali-like influence on Rattigan and persuaded the pacifist playwright to join the RAF as a means of curing his writer's block. Oddly, this unorthodox treatment seemed to have some effect; by 1941, Rattigan was writing again. On one dramatic sea crossing, an engine failed, and with everyone forced to jettison all excess baggage and possessions, Rattigan threw the hard covers and blank pages from the notebook containing his new play, stuffing the precious manuscript into his jacket.

Rattigan drew on his RAF experiences to write a new play, *Flare Path*. Bronson Albery and Bill Linnit who had supported *French Without Tears* both turned the play down, believing that the last thing that the public wanted was a play about the war.[13] H. M. Tennent Ltd., led by the elegant Hugh 'Binkie' Beaumont, was the third management offered the script; and in 1942, *Flare Path* opened in London, eventually playing almost 700 performances. Meticulously interweaving the stories of three couples against the backdrop of wartime uncertainty, Rattigan found himself 'commended, if not exactly as a professional playwright, at least as a promising apprentice who had definitely begun to learn the rudiments of his job'.[14] Beaumont, already on the way to becoming the most powerful and successful West End producer of the era, was an influential ally for Rattigan. There is a curious side-story to this production; Dr Keith Newman decided to watch 250 performances of this play and write up the insights that his 'serial attendance' had afforded him. George Bernard Shaw remarked that such playgoing behaviour 'would have driven me mad; and I am not sure that [Newman] came out of it without a slight derangement'. Shaw's caution was wise.[15] In late 1945, Newman went insane and eventually died in a psychiatric hospital.

Meanwhile, Rattigan had achieved two more successes; the witty farce, *While the Sun Shines*, and the more serious, though politically clumsy, *Love in Idleness* (retitled *O Mistress Mine* in America). He had also co-written a number of successful films, including *The Day Will Dawn, Uncensored*, *The Way to the Stars* and an adaptation of *French Without Tears*. By the end of 1944, Rattigan had three plays running in the West End, a record only beaten by Somerset Maugham's four in 1908.

Love in Idleness was dedicated to Henry 'Chips' Channon, the Tory MP who had become Rattigan's lover. Channon's otherwise gossipy diaries record their meeting very discreetly:

'I dined with Juliet Duff in her little flat... also there, Sibyl
Colefax and Master Terence Rattigan, and we sparkled over the
Burgundy. I like Rattigan enormously, and feel a new friendship
has begun. He has a flat in Albany.'[16] Tom Driberg's rather less
discreet account fleshes out the story: Channon's 'seduction of
the playwright was almost like the wooing of Danaë by Zeus –
every day the playwright found, delivered to his door, a
splendid present – a case of champagne, a huge pot of caviar, a
Cartier cigarette box in two kinds of gold... In the end, of
course, he gave in, saying apologetically to his friends, "How
can one *not*?".'[17] It was a very different set in which Rattigan
now moved, one that was wealthy and conservative, the very
people he had criticised in *After the Dance*. Rattigan did not
share the complacency of many of his friends, and his next play
revealed a deepening complexity and ambition.

For a long time, Rattigan had nurtured a desire to become
respected as a serious writer; the commercial success of *French
Without Tears* had, however, sustained the public image of
Rattigan as a wealthy, young, light-comedy writer-about-town.[18]
With *The Winslow Boy*, which premiered in 1946, Rattigan
began to turn this image around. In doing so he entered a new
phase as a playwright. As one contemporary critic observed,
this play 'put him at once into the class of the serious and
distinguished writer'.[19] The play, based on the Archer-Shee case
in which a family attempted to sue the Admiralty for a false
accusation of theft against their son, featured some of Rattigan's
most elegantly crafted and subtle characterisation yet. The
famous second curtain, when the barrister Robert Morton
subjects Ronnie Winslow to a vicious interrogation before
announcing that 'The boy is plainly innocent. I accept the
brief', brought a joyous standing ovation on the first night. No
less impressive is the subtle handling of the concept of 'justice'
and 'rights' through the play of ironies which pits Morton's
liberal complacency against Catherine Winslow's feminist
convictions.

Two years later, Rattigan's *Playbill*, comprising the one-act
plays *The Browning Version* and *Harlequinade*, showed an ever
deepening talent. The latter is a witty satire of the kind of
touring theatre encouraged by the new Committee for the

Encouragement of Music and Arts (CEMA, the immediate forerunner of the Arts Council). But the former's depiction of a failed, repressed Classics teacher evinced an ability to choreograph emotional subtleties on stage that outstripped anything Rattigan had yet demonstrated.

Adventure Story, which in 1949 followed hard on the heels of *Playbill*, was less successful. An attempt to dramatise the emotional dilemmas of Alexander the Great, Rattigan seemed unable to escape the vernacular of his own circle, and the epic scheme of the play sat oddly with Alexander's more prosaic concerns.

Rattigan's response to both the critical bludgeoning of this play and the distinctly lukewarm reception of *Playbill* on Broadway was to write a somewhat extravagant article for the *New Statesman*. 'Concerning the Play of Ideas' was a desire to defend the place of 'character' against those who would insist on the pre-eminence in drama of ideas.[20] The essay is not clear and is couched in such teasing terms that it is at first difficult to see why it should have secured such a fervent response. James Bridie, Benn Levy, Peter Ustinov, Sean O'Casey, Ted Willis, Christopher Fry and finally George Bernard Shaw all weighed in to support or condemn the article. Finally Rattigan replied in slightly more moderate terms to these criticisms insisting (and the first essay reasonably supports this) that he was not calling for the end of ideas in the theatre, but rather for their inflection through character and situation.[21] However, the damage was done (as, two years later, with his 'Aunt Edna', it would again be done). Rattigan was increasingly being seen as the arch-proponent of commercial vacuity.[22]

The play Rattigan had running at the time added weight to his opponents' charge. Originally planned as a dark comedy, *Who is Sylvia?* became a rather more frivolous thing both in the writing and the playing. Rattled by the failure of *Adventure Story*, and superstitiously aware that the new play was opening at the Criterion, where fourteen years before *French Without Tears* had been so successful, Rattigan and everyone involved in the production had steered it towards light farce and obliterated the residual seriousness of the original conceit.

Rattigan had ended his affair with Henry Channon and taken up with Kenneth Morgan, a young actor who had appeared in *Follow My Leader* and the film of *French Without Tears*. However, the relationship had not lasted and Morgan had for a while been seeing someone else. Rattigan's distress was compounded one day in February 1949, when he received a message that Morgan had killed himself. Although horrified, Rattigan soon began to conceive an idea for a play. Initially it was to have concerned a homosexual relationship, but Beaumont, his producer, persuaded him to change the relationship to a heterosexual one.[23] At a time when the Lord Chamberlain refused to allow any plays to be staged that featured homosexuality, such a proposition would have been a commercial impossibility. The result is one of the finest examples of Rattigan's craft. The story of Hester Collyer, trapped in a relationship with a man incapable of returning her love, and her transition from attempted suicide to groping, uncertain self-determination is handled with extraordinary economy, precision and power. The depths of despair and desire that Rattigan plumbs have made *The Deep Blue Sea* one of his most popular and moving pieces.

1953 saw Rattigan's romantic comedy *The Sleeping Prince*, planned as a modest, if belated, contribution to the Coronation festivities. However, the project was hypertrophied by the insistent presence of Laurence Olivier and Vivien Leigh in the cast and the critics were disturbed to see such whimsy from the author of *The Deep Blue Sea*.

Two weeks after its opening, the first two volumes of Rattigan's *Collected Plays* were published. The preface to the second volume introduced one of Rattigan's best-known, and most notorious creations: Aunt Edna. 'Let us invent,' he writes, 'a character, a nice respectable, middle-class, middle-aged, maiden lady, with time on her hands and the money to help her pass it.'[24] Rattigan paints a picture of this eternal theatregoer, whose bewildered disdain for modernism ('Picasso – "those dreadful reds, my dear, and why three noses?"')[25] make up part of the particular challenge of dramatic writing. The intertwined commercial and cultural pressures that the audience brings with it exert considerable force on the playwright's work.

Rattigan's creation brought considerable scorn upon his head.
But Rattigan is neither patronising nor genuflecting towards
Aunt Edna. The whole essay is aimed at demonstrating the
crucial role of the audience in the theatrical experience.
Rattigan's own sense of theatre was *learned* as a member of the
audience, and he refuses to distance himself from this woman:
'despite my already self-acknowledged creative ambitions I did
not in the least feel myself a being apart. If my neighbours
gasped with fear for the heroine when she was confronted with
a fate worse than death, I gasped with them'.[26] But equally, he
sees his job as a writer to engage in a gentle tug-of-war with the
audience's expectations: 'although Aunt Edna must never be
made mock of, or bored, or befuddled, she must equally not be
wooed, or pandered to or cosseted'.[27] The complicated relation
between satisfying and surprising this figure may seem
contradictory, but as Rattigan notes, 'Aunt Edna herself is
indeed a highly contradictory character.'[28]

But Rattigan's argument, as in the 'Play of Ideas' debate before
it, was taken to imply an insipid pandering to the unchallenging
expectations of his audience. Aunt Edna dogged his career from
that moment on and she became such a byword for what theatre
should *not* be that in 1960, the Questors Theatre, Ealing, could
title a triple-bill of Absurdist plays, 'Not For Aunt Edna'.[29]

Rattigan's next play did help to restore his reputation as a
serious dramatist. *Separate Tables* was another double-bill,
set in a small Bournemouth hotel. The first play develops
Rattigan's familiar themes of sexual longing and humiliation
while the second pits a man found guilty of interfering with
women in a local cinema against the self-appointed moral jurors
in the hotel. The evening was highly acclaimed and the
subsequent Broadway production a rare American success.

However, Rattigan's reign as the leading British playwright was
about to be brought to an abrupt end. In a car from Stratford to
London, early in 1956, Rattigan spent two and a half hours
informing his Oxford contemporary George Devine why the
new play he had discovered would not work in the theatre.
When Devine persisted, Rattigan answered 'Then I know
nothing about plays.' To which Devine replied, 'You know

everything about plays, but you don't know a fucking thing about *Look Back in Anger*.'[30] Rattigan only barely attended the first night. He and Hugh Beaumont wanted to leave at the interval until the critic T. C. Worsley persuaded them to stay.[31]

The support for the English Stage Company's initiative was soon overwhelming. Osborne's play was acclaimed by the influential critics Kenneth Tynan and Harold Hobson, and the production was revived frequently at the Court, soon standing as the banner under which that disparate band of men (and women), the Angry Young Men, would assemble. Like many of his contemporaries, Rattigan decried the new movements, Beckett and Ionesco's turn from Naturalism, the wild invective of Osborne, the passionate socialism of Wesker, the increasing influence of Brecht. His opposition to them was perhaps intemperate, but he knew what was at stake: 'I may be prejudiced, but I'm pretty sure it won't survive,' he said in 1960, 'I'm prejudiced because if it *does* survive, I know I won't.'[32]

Such was the power and influence of the new movement that Rattigan almost immediately seemed old-fashioned. And from now on, his plays began to receive an almost automatic panning. His first play since *Separate Tables* (1954) was *Variation on a Theme* (1958). But between those dates the critical mood had changed. To make matters worse, there was the widely publicised story that nineteen-year-old Shelagh Delaney had written the successful *A Taste of Honey* in two weeks after having seen *Variation on a Theme* and deciding that she could do better. A more sinister aspect of the response was the increasingly open accusation that Rattigan was dishonestly concealing a covert homosexual play within an apparently heterosexual one. The two champions of Osborne's play, Tynan and Hobson, were joined by Gerard Fay in the *Manchester Guardian* and Alan Brien in the *Spectator* to ask 'Are Things What They Seem?'[33]

When he is not being attacked for smuggling furtively homosexual themes into apparently straight plays, Rattigan is also criticised for lacking the courage to 'come clean' about his sexuality, both in his life and in his writing.[34] But neither of these criticisms really hit the mark. On the one hand, it is rather disingenuous to suggest that Rattigan should have 'come out'.

The 1950s were a difficult time for homosexual men. The flight to the Soviet Union of Burgess and Maclean in 1951 sparked off a major witch-hunt against homosexuals, especially those in prominent positions. Cecil Beaton and Benjamin Britten were rumoured to be targets.[35] The police greatly stepped up the investigation and entrapment of homosexuals and prosecutions rose dramatically at the end of the forties, reaching a peak in 1953–4. One of their most infamous arrests for importuning, in October 1953, was that of John Gielgud.[36]

But neither is it quite correct to imply that somehow Rattigan's plays are *really* homosexual. This would be to misunderstand the way that homosexuality figured in the forties and early fifties. Wartime London saw a considerable expansion in the number of pubs and bars where homosexual men (and women) could meet. This network sustained a highly sophisticated system of gestural and dress codes, words and phrases that could be used to indicate one's sexual desires, many of them drawn from theatrical slang. But the illegality of any homosexual activity ensured that these codes could never become *too* explicit, *too* clear. Homosexuality, then, was explored and experienced through a series of semi-hidden, semi-open codes of behaviour; the image of the iceberg, with the greater part of its bulk submerged beneath the surface, was frequently employed.[37] And this image is, of course, one of the metaphors often used to describe Rattigan's own playwriting.

Reaction came in the form of a widespread paranoia about the apparent increase in homosexuality. The fifties saw a major drive to seek out, understand, and often 'cure' homosexuality. The impetus of these investigations was to bring the unspeakable and underground activities of, famously, 'Evil Men' into the open, to make it fully visible. The Wolfenden Report of 1957 was, without doubt, a certain kind of liberalising document in its recommendation that consensual sex between adult men in private be legalised. However the other side of its effect is to reinstate the integrity of those boundaries – private/public, hidden/exposed, homosexual/heterosexual – which homosexuality was broaching. The criticisms of Rattigan are precisely part of this same desire to divide, clarify and expose.

Many of Rattigan's plays were originally written with explicit homosexual characters (*French Without Tears*, *The Deep Blue Sea* and *Separate Tables*, for example), which he then changed.[38] But many more of them hint at homosexual experiences and activities: the relationship between Tony and David in *First Episode*, the Major in *Follow My Leader* who is blackmailed over an incident in Baghdad ('After all,' he explains, 'a chap's only human, and it was a deuced hot night – '),[39] the suspiciously polymorphous servicemen of *While the Sun Shines*, Alexander the Great and T. E. Lawrence from *Adventure Story* and *Ross*, Mr Miller in *The Deep Blue Sea* and several others. Furthermore, rumours of Rattigan's own bachelor life circulated fairly widely. As indicated above, Rattigan always placed great trust in the audiences of his plays, and it was the audience that had to decode and reinterpret these plays. His plays cannot be judged by the criterion of 'honesty' and 'explicitness' that obsessed a generation after Osborne. They are plays which negotiate sexual desire through structures of hint, implications and metaphor. As David Rudkin has suggested, 'the craftsmanship of which we hear so much loose talk seems to me to arise from deep psychological necessity, a drive to organise the energy that arises out of his own pain. Not to batten it down but to invest it with some expressive clarity that speaks immediately to people, yet keeps itself hidden.'[40]

The shifts in the dominant view of both homosexuality and the theatre that took place in the fifties account for the brutal decline of Rattigan's career. He continued writing, and while *Ross* (1960) was reasonably well received, his ill-judged musical adaptation of *French Without Tears*, *Joie de Vivre* (1960), was a complete disaster, not assisted by a liberal bout of laryngitis among the cast, and the unexpected insanity of the pianist.[41] It ran for four performances.

During the sixties, Rattigan was himself dogged with ill-health: pneumonia and hepatitis were followed by leukaemia. When his death conspicuously failed to transpire, this last diagnosis was admitted to be incorrect. Despite this, he continued to write, producing the successful television play *Heart to Heart* in 1962, and the stage play *Man and Boy* the following year, which received the same sniping that greeted *Variation on a Theme*. In

1964, he wrote *Nelson – a Portrait in Miniature* for Associated Television, as part of a short season of his plays.

It was at this point that Rattigan decided to leave Britain and live abroad. Partly this decision was taken for reasons of health; but partly Rattigan just seemed no longer to be welcome. Ironically, it was the same charge being levelled at Rattigan that he had faced in the thirties, when the newspapers thundered against the those who had supported the Oxford Union's pacifist motion as 'woolly-minded Communists, practical jokers and sexual indeterminates'.[42] As he confessed in an interview late in his life, 'Overnight almost, we were told we were old-fashioned and effete and corrupt and finished, and… I somehow accepted Tynan's verdict and went off to Hollywood to write film scripts.'[43] In 1967 he moved to Bermuda as a tax exile. A stage adaptation of his Nelson play, as *Bequest to the Nation*, had a lukewarm reception.

Rattigan had a bad sixties, but his seventies seemed to indicate a turnaround in his fortunes and reputation. At the end of 1970, a successful production of *The Winslow Boy* was the first of ten years of acclaimed revivals. In 1972, Hampstead Theatre revived *While the Sun Shines*, and a year later the Young Vic was praised for its *French Without Tears*. In 1976 and 1977 *The Browning Version* was revived at the King's Head and *Separate Tables* at the Apollo. Rattigan briefly returned to Britain in 1971, pulled partly by his renewed fortune and partly by the fact that he was given a knighthood in the New Year's honours list. Another double-bill followed in 1973: *In Praise of Love* comprised the weak *Before Dawn* and the moving tale of emotional concealment and creativity, *After Lydia*. Critical reception was more respectful than usual, although the throwaway farce of the first play detracted from the quality of the second.

Cause Célèbre, commissioned by BBC Radio and others, concerned the Rattenbury case, in which Alma Rattenbury's aged husband was beaten to death by her eighteen-year-old lover. Shortly after its radio premiere, Rattigan was diagnosed with bone cancer. Rattigan's response, having been through the false leukaemia scare in the early sixties, was to greet the news with unruffled elegance, welcoming the opportunity to 'work harder and indulge myself more'.[44] The hard work included a play about the Asquith family and a stage adaptation of *Cause Célèbre*, but, as production difficulties began to arise over the latter, the Asquith play slipped out of Rattigan's grasp. Although very ill, he returned to Britain, and on 4 July 1977, he was taken by limousine from his hospital bed to Her Majesty's Theatre, where he watched his last ever premiere. A fortnight later he had a car drive him around the West End where two of his plays were then running before boarding the plane for the last time. On 30 November 1977, in Bermuda, he died.

As Michael Billington's perceptive obituary noted, 'his whole work is a sustained assault on English middle-class values: fear of emotional commitment, terror in the face of passion, apprehension about sex'.[45] In death, Rattigan began once again to be seen as someone critically opposed to the values with which he had so long been associated, a writer dramatising dark moments of bleak compassion and aching desire.

Notes

1. Quoted in Rattigan's *Daily Telegraph* obituary (1 December 1977).

2. Michael Darlow and Gillian Hodson. *Terence Rattigan: The Man and His Work*. London and New York: Quartet Books, 1979, p. 26.

3. See, for example, Sheridan Morley. 'Terence Rattigan at 65.' *The Times*. (9 May 1977).

4. Terence Rattigan. Preface. *The Collected Plays of Terence Rattigan: Volume Two*. London: Hamish Hamilton, 1953, p. xv.

5. *Ibid.*, p. viii.

6. *Ibid.*, p. vii.

7. *Ibid.*, p. vii.

8. cf. Sheridan Morley, *op. cit.*

9. Humphrey Carpenter. *OUDS: A Centenary History of the Oxford University Dramatic Society*. With a Prologue by Robert Robinson. Oxford: Oxford University Press, 1985, p. 123.

10. Rattigan may well have reprised this later in life. John Osborne, in his autobiography, recalls a friend showing him a picture of Rattigan performing in an RAF drag show: 'He showed me a photograph of himself with Rattigan, dressed in a *tutu*, carrying a wand, accompanied by a line of aircraftsmen, during which Terry had sung his own show-stopper, 'I'm just about the oldest fairy in the business. I'm quite the oldest fairy that you've ever seen''.' John Osborne. *A Better Class of Person: An Autobiography, Volume I 1929–1956*. London: Faber and Faber, 1981, p. 223.

11. Darlow and Hodson *op. cit.*, p. 83.

12. Norman Gwatkin. Letter to Gilbert Miller, 28 July 1938. in: *Follow My Leader*. Lord Chamberlain's Correspondence: LR 1938. [British Library].

13. Richard Huggett. *Binkie Beaumont: Eminence Grise of the West Theatre 1933–1973*. London: Hodder & Stoughton, 1989, p. 308.

14. Terence Rattigan. Preface. *The Collected Plays of Terence Rattigan: Volume One*. London: Hamish Hamilton, 1953, p. xiv.

15. George Bernard Shaw, in: Keith Newman. *Two Hundred and Fifty Times I Saw a Play: or, Authors, Actors and Audiences*. With the facsimile of a comment by Bernard Shaw. Oxford: Pelagos Press, 1944, p. 2.

16. Henry Channon. *Chips: The Diaries of Sir Henry Channon*. Edited by Robert Rhodes James. Harmondsworth: Penguin, 1974, p. 480. Entry for 29 September 1944.

17. Tom Driberg. *Ruling Passions*. London: Jonathan Cape, 1977, p. 186.

18. See, for example, Norman Hart. 'Introducing Terence Rattigan,' *Theatre World*. xxxi, 171. (April 1939). p. 180 or Ruth Jordan. 'Another Adventure Story,' *Woman's Journal*. (August 1949), pp. 31–32.

19. Audrey Williamson. *Theatre of Two Decades*. New York and London: Macmillan, 1951, p. 100.

20. Terence Rattigan. 'Concerning the Play of Ideas,' *New Statesman and Nation*. (4 March 1950), pp. 241–242.

21 Terence Rattigan. 'The Play of Ideas,' *New Statesman and Nation*. (13 May 1950), pp. 545–546. See also Susan Rusinko, 'Rattigan versus Shaw: The 'Drama of Ideas' Debate'. in: *Shaw: The Annual of Bernard Shaw Studies: Volume Two*. Edited by Stanley Weintraub. University Park, Penn: Pennsylvania State University Press, 1982. pp. 171–78.

22. John Elsom writes that Rattigan's plays 'represented establishment writing'. *Post-War British Drama*. Revised Edition. London: Routledge, 1979, p. 33.

23. B. A. Young. *The Rattigan Version: Sir Terence Rattigan and the Theatre of Character*. Hamish Hamilton: London, 1986, pp. 102–103; and Darlow and Hodson, *op. cit.*, p. 196, 204n.

24. Terence Rattigan. *Coll. Plays: Vol. Two. op. cit.*, pp. xi–xii.

25. *Ibid.*, p. xii.

26. *Ibid.*, p. xiv.

27. *Ibid.*, p. xvi.

28. *Ibid.*, p. xviii.

29. Opened on 17 September 1960. cf. *Plays and Players*. vii, 11 (November 1960).

30. Quoted in Irving Wardle. *The Theatres of George Devine*. London: Jonathan Cape, 1978, p. 180.

31. John Osborne. *Almost a Gentleman: An Autobiography, Volume II 1955–1966*. London: Faber and Faber, 1991, p. 20.

32. Robert Muller. 'Soul-Searching with Terence Rattigan.' *Daily Mail.* (30 April 1960).

33. The headline of Hobson's review in the *Sunday Times*, 11 May 1958.

34. See, for example, Nicholas de Jongh. *Not in Front of the Audience: Homosexuality on Stage*. London: Routledge, 1992, pp. 55–58.

35. Kathleen Tynan. *The Life of Kenneth Tynan*. Corrected Edition. London: Methuen, 1988, p. 118.

36. Cf. Jeffrey Weeks. *Coming Out: Homosexual Politics in Britain from the Nineteenth Century to the Present*. Revised and Updated Edition. London and New York: Quartet, 1990, p. 58; Peter Wildeblood. *Against the Law*. London: Weidenfeld and Nicolson, 1955, p. 46. The story of Gielgud's arrest may be found in Huggett, *op. cit.*, pp. 429–431. It was Gielgud's arrest which apparently inspired Rattigan to write the second part of *Separate Tables*, although again, thanks this time to the Lord Chamberlain, Rattigan had to change the Major's offence to a heterosexual one. See Darlow and Hodson, *op. cit.*, p. 228.

37. See, for example, Rodney Garland's novel about homosexual life in London, *The Heart in Exile*. London: W. H. Allen, 1953, p. 104.

38. See note 36; and also 'Rattigan Talks to John Simon,' *Theatre Arts*. 46 (April 1962), p. 24.

39. Terence Rattigan and Anthony Maurice. *Follow My Leader.* Typescript. Lord Chamberlain Play Collection: 1940/2. Box 2506. [British Library].

40. Quoted in Darlow and Hodson, *op. cit.*, p. 15.

41. B. A. Young, *op. cit.*, p. 162.

42. Quoted in Darlow and Hodson, *op. cit.*, p. 56.

43. Quoted in Sheridan Morley, *op. cit.*

44. Darlow and Hodson, *op. cit.*, p. 308.

45. *Guardian*. (2 December 1977).

Cause Célèbre

Late Sunday evening, on 24 March 1935, the local family GP, Dr William O'Donnell, was surprised to receive an emergency call to visit the Villa Madeira, on Manor Road, Bournemouth. He had often been to the house to attend to Alma Rattenbury, who had been treated for a tubercular condition three years before, and also to visit her rather older husband, the respected architect Francis Rattenbury.[1]

When he arrived at the house shortly after 11.00 p.m., he discovered Francis slumped unconscious in a chair, his hair matted with blood, a bloodstained towel wrapped around his head. A surgeon, Dr Rooke, was called and confirmed that Francis had suffered three heavy blows to the side of the head. Alma meanwhile was distracted, confused, a large glass of whisky in her hand. Her attempts to help the surgeon were clumsy; 'If you want to kill your husband,' he told her, 'you're going the best way about it.'

At around 2.00 a.m., a PC Bagwell arrived to examine what was now clearly a crime scene. He found Alma very drunk, playing gramophone records loudly, dancing and offering first to kiss him, then to bribe him. And then she stopped, blurting out a confession: 'I did it, with a mallet.'

Francis Rattenbury – known to his friends as 'Ratz' – was already in his late fifties when he met and married Alma Pakenham, a gifted pianist in her twenties. Francis and Alma were both married when they met, Alma on her second husband, but neither their respective spouses nor the difference in their ages were barriers to what was at first a relationship of mutual love, support and respect. Francis had spent most of his working life in Canada where he met Alma, but they both shared a desire to settle down together in England, eventually deciding to rent the Villa Madeira in Bournemouth. With Francis's support, Alma forged a small-scale career as a songwriter under the name 'Lozanne'.

Their relationship cooled fairly quickly in Bournemouth. Francis was increasingly given to depressive episodes in which he would talk of suicide. He still worked, but without enthusiasm. In 1934, he decided that he no longer wanted to drive, and they agreed to advertise for a driver and odd-job man. The young man they hired was eighteen-year-old George Stoner.

Just as the difference in ages had not stopped Alma falling for Francis, it did not stop George falling for his new employer, and soon Alma and George had embarked on an affair. She and Francis were no longer having sex and it may have been that he was aware of the relationship and tacitly accepted it. In March 1935, she asked Francis for £250, on a spurious pretext, so she could visit London with George. They stayed at The Royal Palace Hotel, visited theatres and cinemas, and went on a spending spree in Harrods, where George was kitted out with silk pyjamas, a suit, shirts and shoes; he chose a ring for Alma. By now, George was living in at the Villa Madeira.

But George was a jealous and fearful lover. More than once Alma made to break off their relationship, but George threatened to kill her or himself. He claimed that he was a cocaine user, that he carried around a blade. Alma seemed thrilled by her bad boy and the relationship continued.

On 24 March 1935, Francis was in a very deep gloom. To cheer him up, Alma had tea with him in his bedroom and suggested that they go and stay with a friend of theirs and made the arrangements herself, which seemed briefly to lift his spirits. This all seems to have enraged George, who cornered her, demanding that she never again go in Ratz's bedroom with the door closed and that they must not visit their friend. He was furious at the thought that Alma and her husband might share a bed while he, the driver, would sleep alone and separately. That evening he went to his parents' home and borrowed a mallet.

That night, Alma's companion-help Irene Riggs arrived home late. She heard stertorous breathing but could not tell where it was coming from. Going to her room, she found George on the upstairs landing looking over the banister. Ten minutes after she'd retired to bed, she heard Alma screaming, 'Someone has hurt Ratz!'

After Alma was arrested for Ratz's murder, George seems to have been troubled by guilt. He drank heavily and apparently confessed to Irene that he had borrowed the mallet to put Francis out of the way. He took a train to London in an unsuccessful attempt to find Alma and give himself up. Meanwhile, Irene had confessed what she knew to Dr O'Donnell, who immediately called the police and they intercepted George when he arrived back in Bournemouth that evening.

When the trial opened in late May 1935, the newspaper coverage had ensured a huge and hungry crowd, determined to see Alma hanged. As the contemporary writer F. Tennyson Jesse remarked:

> There was probably no one in England, and no one in court when the trial opened, save Mrs Rattenbury, her solicitor and counsel, Stoner and his solicitor and counsel, and Irene Riggs, who did not think Mrs Rattenbury was guilty of the crime of murder. In everyone's mind, including that of this Editor, there was this picture of Mrs Rattenbury as a coarse, brawling, drunken and callous woman. But life is not as simple as that.[2]

And so it proved. Both defendants maintained their guilt, but it was Alma that broke first, testifying in the witness box that George had come to her room that evening and confessed to murdering her husband. Alma's poise and calm in the witness box impressed many in the court. George's defence, that he had murdered Francis under the influence of cocaine, fell apart when it became clear that George couldn't even identify the colour of cocaine.

After confounding evidence by doctors and policemen, relatives and friends of the accused, the jury delivered their verdict: George Stoner was guilty of Ratz's murder and Alma was to be freed. Though the jury asked for clemency, the Judge had no option but to sentence George to death. Alma, in a state of shock, was smuggled out of the court buildings to avoid a large and angry crowd. She was pursued across London by press and public, taking refuge in a Bayswater nursing home. Two days later, she took a train from Waterloo to Bournemouth but got off at Christchurch. There, on a bank by the River Avon, she wrote a series of fragmentary notes, then took a knife and stabbed herself with a series of frenzied blows. The coroner recorded that 'the left lung had been punctured in four places, and there were three wounds in the heart, one where the instrument had passed more than once'.[3]

The next day, back in London, a young man of twenty-four was on a bus on Park Lane and saw the headline: 'Mrs Rattenbury Kills Herself'.

> I thought then... as a budding playwright... My God, what a revenge on her detractors, of whom God knows I was one. I was with everybody else in thinking she was the bitch of all time... I couldn't use it then, but I thought one day I could have a shot at it.[4]

The playwright was Terence Rattigan, still over a year away from his breakthrough success, *French Without Tears*. Indeed, it would be forty years until he returned to this story and the result would be his last play, and one of his finest.

In the late fifties and through the sixties, Rattigan had fallen steeply from fashion, but the seventies saw a return to form and favour, with a string of successful revivals (see pp. xviii–xix), and the first good reviews for a new play in over a decade for *In Praise of Love* (1973). This latter play was an elegant restatement, but with new intensity, of Rattigan's belief in the virtues of emotional restraint, the theatrical and personal power of indirection and the unspoken. His next play would be, in some ways, the opposite: a defiant defence of sexual desire, emotional honesty, and a ferocious attack on the moral pieties of middle-class, middle-brow Middle England.

Cause Célèbre began its life on the radio. Rattigan had been writing a television play for the BBC on the subject of the dancer Vaslav Nijinsky, and the bisexual triangle between him, Sergei Diaghilev, and Romola de Pulszky, who eventually married the young man. Romola, who was still alive, objected to the portrait and Rattigan, unwilling to take the case to court, backed down; the script was never made.[5] Deeply disappointed by the collapse of a cherished project, he gladly accepted the commission to write a radio play, and for his subject he turned to the trial that had obsessed him forty years before. The play had several titles – *Crime Passionelle*, *Come to Judgement*, and *A Woman of Principle* – before he chose *Cause Célèbre*.[6]

Much of the radio play – and the stage play that it would later become – is drawn directly from the real events of 1935. Some parts of the play may be regarded fairly as a kind of documentary theatre; the flashbacks to the night of the murder are taken directly from witness testimony; key exchanges in the trial scenes reflect the court transcript; and Alma's final speech of the play is only lightly edited from her own final letters.

But this is not pure documentary. As he wrote in the introductory notes to the producer of the radio script, 'it was not a documentary that you required, but a play'.[7] To that end, he made a series of crucial changes to the historical record to create his play. Most notably, he introduces an entirely fictional parallel plot, concerning a Mrs Davenport who is called for jury service and, despite a deep moral prejudice against Mrs Rattenbury, finally votes 'not guilty', the truth overwhelming hatred at the last. Furthermore, Rattigan is keen to ensure that a focus on the drama of the trial's defendants is balanced with a broader social perspective that shows the reporting of the case and the ugliness of public reaction to the events.

This is not, however, a facsimile recreation of a legal curiosity; it is in fact one of Rattigan's most personal, indeed autobiographical, plays. Mrs Davenport lives in a small hotel in West Kensington, the exact location that he had given for Aunt Edna, his most notorious and misunderstood creation, a force for conservatism with whom the playwright must do battle.[8] But the connection may be even more personal. In the radio play, Mrs Davenport's address is given as The Cornwall Gardens Hotel. Cornwall Gardens is the West Kensington street where Rattigan was born, the home of his mother, Vera Rattigan, of whom Edith Davenport – count the syllables – may be a coded portrait. Like Vera, Edith comes from a family of lawyers, and her marriage is in tatters after a string of her husband's affairs, a situation that recalls Frank Rattigan's philandering. Vera had died four years earlier in 1971. Terry had always been a devoted son, but in the last years their relationship had deteriorated, perhaps because he had ceased to conceal his homosexuality in her presence. Vera had become, in some ways, a figure of judgemental moralism and so was her avatar in this play.

Rattigan admitted that during the trial he had joined in the general condemnation, but on the discovery of her suicide had begun a slow journey – like Mrs Davenport – towards sympathy and identification. Rattigan would be fifty-six years old by the time homosexual acts were decriminalised and lived for most of his adult life in an atmosphere of suspicion and fear of exposure. Alma was, as F. Tennyson Jesse remarked, a victim of 'that worst of all Anglo-Saxon attitudes, a contemptuous condemnation of the man and woman, but more particularly the woman, unfortunate enough to be found out in sexual delinquency'.[9] The homophony between the names 'Rattenbury' and 'Rattigan' betokens a deeper connection between their two experiences. The people who persecuted Alma Rattenbury were the very people who would persecute Rattigan and his fellow homosexuals.

The autobiographical connections do not end there. Mrs Davenport has a son, Tony. In the radio play, it is suggested quite clearly that he is having some kind of romantic relationship with another boy at the school, a Vietnamese Prince Phen Lon. In a misguided attempt to gain heterosexual experience, he pays for a prostitute. In the stage version, he contracts a sexually transmitted disease. Rattigan claimed this, too, was autobiographical, though at least one of his biographers doubts this.[10] Perhaps the radio script is closer to the truth: here, the boy goes back to a room with the woman, but fails to achieve an erection.

The play arraigns the forces of repression against Alma's singular sexuality. Mrs Davenport's puritan condemnation is amplified by the appearance in the play of the hostile mob: at one point, greeting Alma's arrival at court, Rattigan gives the chilling direction '*a frenzied scream of collective rage*'.[11] It is also made clear what has stoked this hatred: the play offers a vivid picture of the press's salacious interest and persistent misreporting of the trial. For example, when we hear George and Alma enter their pleas, George sounds confident and Alma hesitant, though reporters phone in stories of her brazenness and his timidity. Rattigan's radio script is rather long and some of the press scenes had been deleted by the time the play was broadcast. The language of the courtroom, with its casual misogynistic contempt and its sheer lack of the concern for the real woman, completes a picture of patriarchal judgement that Rattigan implies is in part responsible for her decision to kill herself.

Against this is Alma herself, played on the radio by Diana Dors, a sex symbol of the 1950s with a rather torrid personal life. Dors brings both a tremendous sexuality to the role but also captures Alma's innocence. One of the key features of *Cause Célèbre* that marks it out from many of Rattigan's plays is that it has a protagonist who learns how to tell the truth about herself. Finally, when she testifies in the witness box, it is her utter lack of evasiveness on matters sexual that compels us, her plain comfort with her sexuality that acts as a convincing counter to the forces of piety and prurience.

In truth, when writing the radio play, Rattigan was perhaps still on the journey towards full sympathy for his character. Alma can sometimes seem less straightforward than other-worldly. In the script, Rattigan has moments of mockery for the historical Alma, as in his note about her music:

> Whether any of 'Lozanne's' songs still exist, or whether they have all be[en] consigned to the oblivation [*sic*] which expert musical opinion has claimed they deserve is unknown to the author at the present time. He would anyway suggest that invention would probably be better advised than strict authenticity, and is even heroically prepared to have a shot at a 'Lozanne' lyric (of which all that is known is that they were of a vulgarity, cheapness and sentimentality unsurpassed even in the pop-musical annals) provided a composer will come up with a 'Lozanne' melody [...] The title, used above [He has suggested a song called 'My Life is Like a Spring Flower'] is anyway invented, and we can surely proceed from there and invent the few bars and lines necessary without much danger of producing an unexpected 'top of the pops for 1975'.

He goes on satirically to suggest a song about a 'shower [...] which drove the lovers from the bower to the tower, where they spent a lovely hour'.[12] In the event, the BBC opted to use two of 'Lozanne's' actual songs and they strike the modern listener as simple and uncluttered melodies and lyrics, not quite the idiocies that Rattigan assumes.

Cause Célèbre uses the possibilities of radio with great effect. There are dozens of locations and the fifty or more scenes flow restlessly into one another, following characters on journeys, the proceedings taking on, at times, a hallucinatory character as the language of the law joins forces with moral piety to denounce Alma.

The play was recorded between 22 and 26 September at Broadcasting House, London, directed by veteran BBC radio producer, Norman Wright. Robin Browne played George, an exquisitely frosty Gwen Watford was Mrs Davenport and Gareth Johnson her priggish son. Noel Johnson – the first Dick Barton – played O'Connor, her defence barrister. One last-minute change is that George Stoner became George Wood. It seems likely that Rattigan had assumed that Stoner was dead and, realising he was still living and not wanting another confrontation like that with Romola Nijinska, changed the name. (Indeed, Stoner's death sentence was commuted to a term of imprisonment, from which he was released after seven years. He died in 2000 in a hospital less than half a mile from the riverbank on which Alma killed herself.) The play was broadcast on BBC Radio 4, on 27 October 1975.

One listener to the play was John Gale, an ex-actor and theatrical producer, who liked it very much and contacted Rattigan, asking if he'd consider adapting his play for the stage. Gale had a director, Robert Chetwyn, interested in the piece and thought that Dorothy Tutin might make an excellent Alma. Rattigan wanted very much to see another play of his performed on a West End stage and admired Tutin, but could not work out a way of transferring the elegant fluidity of *Cause Célèbre* to the theatre. He wondered if the parallels and differences between the two central women might be emphasised by having them played by the same actor, but discarded this notion realising that it would mean turning a challenging play into an impossible one.

The path that led *Cause Célèbre* from radio to stage is long and twisting and not easy to follow. It does not help that the archive, usually so carefully arranged, is, for this last play, somewhat disordered. Shortly before Christmas 1975, Rattigan was told that the cancer with which he had been diagnosed three years before had spread to his bones and was now irreversible. Over the next two years Rattigan was increasingly weakened by both his illness and the attempts at treatment. He seems to have taken less care of his papers in that time, and the story of *Cause Célèbre* is less easy to trace.

However, Rattigan tried twice to write a stage version of the play. Neither of these was fully successful. In one version, he moved decisively away from the documentary elements, trying to fit the play into the mid-century theatrical conventions with which he was so familiar. Although there are some touching moments, much of what is poignant in the radio play becomes merely sentimental and weighed down by cumbersome dramaturgical devices. For example, trying to solve the problem of how to show Alma's death on the riverbank – so easy to evoke on radio, less easy to do on stage – he has the dreadful idea of returning her to the Villa Madeira, where she enacts the following implausible sequence of actions:

> *She goes to a dresser and matter-of-factly tries the sharpness of one or two knives, selecting one.*
>
> God give me the courage! Don't let me funk it, like I did with the bus!
>
> *She has opened her mackintosh, and now opens her blouse on the left side, fumbling to find her heart.*
>
> Oh why not? Why not?
>
> *She pulls the curtains a little open.*
>
> Why not do it looking at them?
>
> *She gazes at the unseen flowers for some time.*
>
> Please God – look after my children… And give me the strength – one must have strength – God give me the strength –
>
> *She stabs herself very hard four times in quick succession.*
>
> Not – the right – place – again –

She stabs again.

Yes. That's it. Once more – if I can… Just once more – Oh
God let me – once more – just give me peace –

*She stabs herself for the last time. In falling dead, she pulls
the curtains down from the pelmet boards and they half
cover her lifeless body. From the front door now comes a
loud imperious knocking.*[13]

Even when writing his best plays, Rattigan used drafts to get
bad ideas out of his system.[14] Yet it's clear that the problem is
finding a stage equivalent to the epic fluidity that he'd
discovered when telling his story on the radio.

Rattigan found it difficult working with Robert Chetwyn and
asked him to be replaced, which he was, by Peter Coe.
Unfortunately, Rattigan was not happy with him either. Coe
was delighted by the documentary aspects of the play, but was
quite unconvinced by the Mrs Davenport plot. In addition, his
staging ideas were too extravagant and expensive.[15] In the
meantime, Dorothy Tutin had become unavailable. Without a
script, a director, or a leading lady, the play seemed hopeless,
until Robin Midgley appeared. Midgley was the Artistic
Director of the Leicester Haymarket, which is where he
proposed it open, prior to a London run. Rattigan was
particularly pleased to hear that he thought the play was
certainly stageworthy and that a workable draft was already
there, somewhere in the one radio and two stage scripts
Rattigan had already written.

Midgley arrived in Bermuda with a collage of the three
versions to serve as a starting point for him to help Rattigan
complete a finished script. The playwright was delighted with
his ideas and the two men worked well together for two weeks.
Although Rattigan was ill, they worked for two hours each
morning and two hours each afternoon, Rattigan dictating
scenes, and Midgley taking his notes away and typing them up.
After his return to London, Midgley produced a further
neatened-up copy of the script, to which Rattigan made some
small amendments, and the play went into rehearsal in the
spring of 1977.

Some of the first critics of the play complained that the stage version was rather close to the radio original. Rattigan's friend, the critic B. A. Young, declares flatly that the resultant stage version 'was not very different from the radio play'.[16] This is completely mistaken. Together, Rattigan and Midgley have turned the play inside out, creating certainly the most structurally radical play Rattigan ever wrote. Irving Wardle's review of the premiere describes it as 'a perfectly coherent picture, smashed to fragments and regrouped into a mosaic'.[17]

While the radio play is completely chronological, except for two flashbacks, the stage play leaps backwards and forwards in time, flashing between stories, taking us into Alma and Edith's subjective experiences of the trial, overlaying scenes imagistically on top of one another. There had been hints of this in plays like *Adventure Story*, *Ross* and *Bequest to the Nation*; Rattigan's determination to use theatre lighting to guide our attention and mood is something he had tried a little of in *In Praise of Love*, but here the confidence and boldness is much greater.

Where the former play had been all restraint and understatement, in the stage version Rattigan embraced the shattering and disruptive imagery of the story to offer a theatrical experience that was much more to do with 1977 than 1935. Less than ten years after the abolition of the Lord Chamberlain's censorship of theatre, the landscape of British playwriting had changed utterly. New playwrights like David Hare, Howard Brenton, Edward Bond and Snoo Wilson worked with shocking, unsettling images of juxtaposed violence and sexuality, laughter and aggression: Gethin Price in Trevor Griffiths's *Comedians* (1975) performing a stand-up comedy act of violent class hatred; two Roman legionaries in ancient Britain raping and killing a boy druid in Brenton's *The Romans in Britain* (1980); seventeenth-century Londoners eating a picnic at the foot of a gibbet on which is stretched the dead body of a woman thief in Bond's *Bingo* (1973). These were the new images of British theatre.

As Ncil Bartlett, director of the play's first major revival, points out, Rattigan makes common cause with this new generation in his play:

The key images of the play are as casually shocking as anything else in the drama of the decade; a drunken, barefoot woman vomiting into a pool of her husband's blood; a suicidal teenager choking on a bathroom floor; an unemployed builder dressed up in silk pyjamas from Harrods. Throughout all of this, well-dressed women read *The Times* and well-spoken lawyers pronounce the law, but to no effect. Rattigan's England, in 1976, is not a safe or reassuring place.[18]

The splintered structure of the theatrical *Cause Célèbre* is a vision of a world in moral disarray, its misdirected fury turned not against murder but sexual desire.

Rattigan was determined that his final play – as he described it to friends – would not be dismissed as a museum piece. Thirty years before he had, after all, written a successful play about another celebrated legal case in *The Winslow Boy*. The Archer-Shee trial was a cause célèbre of the Edwardian era, and in writing his version of the story, Rattigan was keen to emulate the theatrical styles of its time. But here he is keen to emphasise that the events of the play are of contemporary significance. In the production notes for the radio play, he states that he has changed the language of the barristers because he didn't want to write a series of 'Robert Mortons' (Morton was eminent QC and star turn of *The Winslow Boy*).[19] He makes almost no attempt to mimic the vocabulary or speech patterns of the 1930s, even though he was working from trial transcripts. Even the gestures towards it in the radio play – the use of the word 'connection' as a thirties legal euphemism for sex – is removed when preparing the stage version. Indeed, his preferred title for the play was *A Woman of Principle*, an elegant title that referred ambiguously to Alma and Edith, but he was so concerned that the play sounded old-fashioned (perhaps thinking of Wilde's *A Woman of No Importance*) that he took the unusual step of writing to two theatre critics – Bernard Levin and Michael Billington – asking 'does it make me too Harley Granville Rattigan for your colleagues?'[20]

Robin Midgley's production was not without its difficulties. The set, designed by Adrian Vaux, was required to serve many functions, and had become, by most accounts, over-elaborate and rather ugly. After Dorothy Tutin had disappeared from the picture, various actors were contemplated, including Joan Plowright, Rachel Roberts, Deborah Kerr. Eventually, and after Rattigan's personal intercession, the part was offered to Glynis Johns, a charismatic film and stage actor who had recently starred in the musical *A Little Night Music* by Stephen Sondheim, who wrote the song 'Send in the Clowns' for her. But during previews at the Leicester Haymarket, Johns became ill and had to pull out from the show, to be replaced by Midgley's partner Heather Sears, a stalwart of the Haymarket company. Charles Gray, who was playing O'Connor, had it in his contract that he was playing opposite Glynis Johns, so when she left, so did he. Rattigan had come to London for the production, his room being in the King Edward VI Hospital for Officers. He was only able to see one performance in Leicester, a painful journey by car up the motorway for a matinee, and another painful journey back down. The play was running rather long, at only ten minutes short of three hours, and some cuts were proposed. By the time it got to London, with Glynis Johns restored, but Charles Gray replaced by the veteran actor (and maverick documentary film-maker) Kenneth Griffith, the signs were not auspicious.

But the critics were largely favourable. Most of the reviews mention Rattigan's ill-health, which had been widely reported, and there was undoubtedly a degree of generosity towards what all knew could be his last play. But also there is recognition in many reviews that perhaps they had been too quick to dismiss him and certainly there is unmistakeable admiration for the boldness of his new dramaturgical form. The play, wrote Bernard Levin, 'betrays no sign of failing powers; on the contrary, it could almost herald a new direction for Sir Terence, and a most interesting direction, too.' 'I have never seen a piece that relied more on flashbacks,' noted Irving Wardle, 'nor one in which this often irritating device is more successful in advancing the action.' Kenneth Griffith was universally admired, Michael Billington putting the point well: 'Kenneth Griffith as Mrs Rattenbury's counsel doesn't so much return to the stage after a long absence as put in a takeover bid.'[21] But the finest reviews were for Glynis Johns who 'begins the evening in silk pyjamas bubbling with sensual invitation and gradually freezes into withdrawn and desperate silence'.[22] According to playwright and critic Frank Marcus, 'the actress takes no short cuts and her expense of energy is phenomenal'.[23]

The praise was not unalloyed. The play was widely felt to have started rather unpromisingly and to have taken a long time to get going. The critics are divided on the Mrs Davenport story, with the *Financial Times*, *New Statesmen* and *Sunday Times* coming out against, and the *Observer*, *The Times* and *Punch* in favour. The set was not much admired. Despite all of Rattigan's efforts, some critics insist on finding in it a 'traditional West End play' and Sheridan Morley even claimed that 'Pinero would have understood *Cause Célèbre* […] so too would Galsworthy and Maugham.'[24]

However, many critics detected more in this than a well-made courtroom drama. It expressed, said Billington, a 'passionate hatred of English Puritanism and noble, unwavering affirmation of life'. John Barber noted it wasn't an example of 'smooth Terence Rattigan technique', but was instead a much more raw play written with 'understanding of sexual love [… and] profound pity for its victims'.[25] Robert Cushman felt similarly: 'Rattigan's celebrated technical mastery usually leaves me cold; here it knocked me out. This is certainly the best of his recent plays; it may be the best of them all.' The play ran more than respectably, clocking up 282 performances, more than any of his plays since *Ross* almost twenty years before.

However, despite strenuous efforts by his agent, the play did not reach Broadway and indeed the play went largely unrevived for twenty years. In 1987, ITV broadcast a television adaptation of the play, starring Helen Mirren as Alma, David Morrissey as George, and David Suchet as O'Connor. It did not reflect particularly well on the play; Mirren gave a listless performance, lacking both passion and torment. David Morrissey was a little old for George, but charted a strong move from confusion to murderous jealousy. The adapter, Ken Taylor, dispensed entirely with Rattigan's jurywoman subplot, reordered the story more conventionally, removed most of Rattigan's dialogue and selection of events, and introduced his own material taken from the original trial.[26]

In 1998, Neil Bartlett directed the first London revival of the play in twenty-one years. It was a production hard on the heels of the Almeida's *The Deep Blue Sea* and Peter Hall's *Separate Tables*, productions that marked a sustained revaluation of Terence Rattigan that has continued to this day. Bartlett, a gay theatre-maker with a particular interest in the sexual underground of mid-century theatre, was entirely in sympathy with Rattigan and thought that in *Cause Célèbre* 'a dark, obsessive and potentially dangerous playwright emerges – one who used the niceties of the London stage as a Trojan Horse from which to savage the city'.[27]

Two decades on, changes in stage technology and the greater familiarity of fluid epic staging meant that Bartlett's production, ably supported by Rae Smith's elegantly weightless design, captured, more surely than the original, the complexity of Rattigan's 'jump-cutting, split-timed, back-tracking, zig-zagging experiment'.[28] Finely cast, with Shakespearean actor Amanda Harris by turns poised, passionate and vulnerable as Alma, was balanced well by Diane Fletcher's tight-lipped and anguished Edith. The play's ferocious assault on conventional moral pieties was recognised by all, Georgina Brown noting that 'Rattigan writes about women with astonishing perception and empathy', and Billington finding in it 'a fitting monument to a subversive theatrical career'. It was a production that rightly established it as one of Rattigan's finest plays: as de Jongh put it, 'one of the most astonishing theatrical swansongs of the English stage this century'.[29]

In 2011, during Rattigan's centenary celebrations, a major new production was mounted at the Old Vic Theatre, directed by Thea Sharrock, fresh from a huge success the previous year reviving *After the Dance* at the National Theatre, which pitted Anne-Marie Duff as Alma against Niamh Cusack as Edith.

Cause Célèbre is a remarkable achievement, demonstrating Rattigan's continuing theatrical vitality and willingness to experiment right to the last. What is most astonishing about it is the control with which he is able to deploy his complex and multilayered structure. We watch much of the first half through Edith Davenport's eyes, the stage appearing to represent her own distorted perspective. After the argument with her son, she is left alone on stage, fulminating about 'That... *that...* woman'. Immediately the stage is transformed into the frenzied crowd waiting to barrack Alma as she arrives at the Old Bailey (pp. 44–45). The second scene flows out of the first, in Neil Bartlett's words, 'as if in insane public amplification of her private emotion'.[30]

In the second act, we are now seeing the world through Alma's eyes; as we move fluently between her testimony in the witness box and flashback, it's almost as if we're experiencing the shattered confusions of her mind. Later, as the barristers sum up, a spotlight fixes on her face as we hear, flowing smoothly together, a series of speeches on all sides, united by cruel sexual contempt; the Judge's words strike hammer-blows as, with Alma, we listen to him describe the jury's most reasonable feelings towards her as 'prejudice, dislike, disapproval, disgust' (p. 99). As Alma is found not guilty, a curious stage direction reads '*The court hears a storm of booing, hissing and shouts of 'Shame!' – but we do not hear it*' (p. 101). The contradiction is only apparent; the public galleries have erupted but we are now hearing these events through Alma's numbed, disbelieving ears. And as the play moves into its final moments, the stories, the time structures are now overlaid entirely on one another: Edith, getting angrily drunk, occupies the same stage as Alma, beside the River Avon, preparing to take her own life; past and future entwine as we watch the Coroner read his report on the suicide that we are watching, and Edith's horrified, ranting reaction – a final shout of rage at a moral world turned upside down – comes in direct response to Alma's final act, the only time in the play when one woman responds directly to the other, though we also know they are days and miles apart.

The moral disarray of the world is beautifully captured by Rattigan in a series of bold and witty theatrical juxtapositions. A society in which people have to hide their feelings, where they adopt poses of moral purity, is caught by a series of elaborate disguises: Alma and Joan have to arrive at court in one another's clothes and get re-attired onstage; immediately this is slyly paralleled by a scene in the lawyer's robing room, as the two courtroom opponents dress and discuss tactics. They even seem to adopt the identities of those they are defending: 'I'd better warn you I intend to push your evil moral influence and your shameless depravity as hard as I can', Casswell tells O'Connor, who retorts, 'I'm going to push your psycho-pathological rages, your surliness and your fits of sudden violence' (p. 48). It is a moment of high theatrical camp, but also part of the play's theatrical depiction of the artifice and dishonesty of this world.

Against that we have Alma, who is perhaps the simplest, most straightforward major character Rattigan ever created. Her answers in the witness box hit a distinct note that we don't hear anywhere else in the play – unadorned, artless honesty about sexual matters:

> O'CONNOR. Since that time you did not live together as husband and wife at all?
>
> ALMA. No.
>
> JUDGE. Mrs Rattenbury, you do understand what was meant by the question?
>
> ALMA. Yes.
>
> O'CONNOR. Did your husband have a separate room?
>
> ALMA. Yes.
>
> O'CONNOR. Was that at his suggestion or yours?
>
> ALMA. Oh, his.
>
> O'CONNOR. You would have been ready to continue marital relations with him?
>
> ALMA, Oh yes, of course. (p. 76)

The lines are unremarkable, but they contrast very strikingly with the legal counsels' rhetorical flights, and Davenport's tangled, puritanical rages.

Where Alma is artless, Rattigan is artful. The play tells an exciting story. One of the changes he has made to his source material is the way he theatricalises Alma's decision to testify. The historical Alma Rattenbury decided to testify against

George before the trial begins. Rattigan has her change her view in two theatrically compelling scenes; in the first, O'Connor confronts her with the consequences of shielding George by bringing in her young son. This horrifies Alma but she has not yet determined to change her mind: her final line of Act One – 'Don't think you've won, Mr O'Connor' (p. 56) – is a powerful declaration of her principled stand and sets the tone for the second act. And then, in the strongest departure from the historical record, O'Connor calls Alma to the witness box, not knowing if she will agree to testify against George. It is an electrifying moment in the play, as Bernard Levin remarked of the premiere, both O'Connor's victory and Alma's defeat, her survival and her own death: 'as the walls crumble about her, the play rises to the level of real tragedy, and the sense of waste is pressed home like a dagger'.[31]

It is hard not to read Alma's final speech in the play as Rattigan's farewell to the world. He has taken it very directly from Alma's final letters. Compare Alma Rattenbury's version:

> Eight o'clock, and after so much walking I have got here [...] And how singular I should have chosen the spot Stoner said he nearly jumped out of the train once at [...] It is beautiful here. What a lovely world, really. It must be easier to be hanged than to do the job oneself, especially under the circumstances of being watched all the time. Pray God nothing stops me tonight... God bless my children and look after them [...] One must be bold to do a thing like this. It is beautiful here, and I am alone. Thank God for peace at last.[32]

with Rattigan's:

> Eight o'clock. After so much running and walking I have got here. I should find myself just at this spot, where George and I once made love. It is beautiful here. What a lovely world we are in, if only we would let ourselves see it. It must be easier to be hanged than to have to do the job oneself. But that's just my bad luck. Pray God nothing stops me. God bless my children and look after them. One has to be bold to do this thing. But it is beautiful here, and I am alone. Thank God for peace at last. (p. 107)

The speeches are very similar, but Rattigan's edits and substitutions are very effective. The speech is simpler, more resigned. The place becomes not associated with threats of suicide, but of sex and love. And, in the middle of it, Alma's 'What a lovely world, really' becomes Rattigan's aching 'What a lovely world we are in, if only we would let ourselves see it', a line that we have heard, in variant forms, twice before in the play. As the darkness of the world closes around her, the line becomes ironic in its mismatch to the hatred we have seen, but it also stands defiantly as Rattigan's utopian affirmation of the irreducibility of love.

Rattigan was taken by car on a tour of the West End where so many of his plays had enjoyed such famous successes, then he returned to Bermuda, where he contracted meningitis. Although he recovered, he was clearly very frail. On 30 November 1977, at midday, with a friend beside him and without fuss, he quietly died. The next night, at the end of the curtain call for *Cause Célèbre*, Glynis Johns stepped forward and asked the audience to join her in three cheers for the play's author. 'We decided against standing in silence,' she explained. 'He was, after all, a man who liked applause.'[33]

DAN REBELLATO

Notes

1 . This account of the life and death of Francis and Alma Rattenbury is taken from three main sources: The Rt. Hon The Lord Havers, Peter Shankland, and Anthony Barrett's *The Rattenbury Case*. Harmondsworth: Penguin, 1989, David Napley's *Murder at the Villa Madeira*. London: Weidenfeld and Nicolson, 1988 and F. Tennyson Jesse's. *Trial of Alma Victoria Rattenbury and George Percy Stoner*. London: William Hodge, 1935, which is rather old but has the additional interest of being the source from which Rattigan took his information.

2. Jesse, *op. cit.*, p. 3.

3. Havers, *op. cit.*, p. 222.

4. Quoted in Geoffrey Wansell. *Terence Rattigan: A Biography*. London: Fourth Estate, 1995, p. 382.

5. Indeed the script remained unpublished and unproduced until 2011, when the Chichester Festival Theatre announced plans for *Rattigan's Nijinsky*, an adaptation by Nicholas Wright, which blends together the unproduced script with the story of its non-production.

6. B. A. Young. *The Rattigan Version: Sir Terence Rattigan and the Theatre of Character*. London: Hamish Hamilton, 1986, pp. 195–6.

7. Terence Rattigan. *Cause Célèbre*. [radio script, 1975] Rattigan Papers: British Library. MSS. Add. 74510. p. 2.

8. Terence Rattigan. *The Collected Plays: Volume Two*. London: Hamish Hamilton, 1953, p. xii.

9. Jesse, *op. cit.*, p. 4.

10. Wansell, *op. cit.*, p. 391.

11. Rattigan. *Cause Célèbre* [radio script, 1975], *op. cit.*, p. 83.

12. *Ibid.*, p. 11. He has probably borrowed his opinion from F. Tennyson Jesse who describes her songs as 'appalling… cheap little lyrics of the more obvious variety' *op. cit.*, p. 8.

13. Terence Rattigan. *Cause Célèbre* [1976 (listed as 1977, but I think it must be earlier)]. Rattigan Papers: British Library. MSS. Add. 74515. pp. 225–227.

14. See, for example, my introduction to *The Deep Blue Sea*. London: Nick Hern, 1999, p. xviii, to see how even his finest play had to pass through choppy and melodramatic waters.

15. Letter. Jan Van Loewen to Terence Rattigan. 20 July 1976. In: *Cause Célèbre* Correspondence. Rattigan Papers: British Library. MSS. Add. 74518.

16. Young, *op. cit.*, p. 197.

17. Irving Wardle. 'New life in courtroom drama'. Review. *The Times*. 5 July 1977. All reviews of 1977 production taken from Production File: *Cause Célèbre*, Her Majesty's Theatre, July 1977. V&A Blythe House Archive.

18. Neil Bartlett. 'Anarchy in the UK' *Cause Célèbre: Programme*. Lyric Hammersmith, 1998.

19. Rattigan. *Cause Célèbre* [radio script, 1975], *op. cit.*, p. 1.

20. Draft of [telegram] to Bernard Levin. Sent 9 March [1977]. In: *Cause Célèbre* Correspondence. Rattigan Papers: British Library. MSS. Add. 74518. Harley Granville Barker was a leading exponent of the Edwardian well-made play. (In his letter to Billington, in the same file and sent the same day, he adds 'Of course bestest title would be *Crime and Punishment* only some Russian blighter seems to have got there first.')

21. Bernard Levin. 'Rattigan's act of defiance'. Review. *Sunday Times*. 10 July 1977; Wardle, *op. cit.*; Michael Billington. Review. *Guardian*. 5 July 1977.

22. Wardle, *op. cit.*

23. Frank Marcus. 'The Master of Flaws'. *Sunday Telegraph*. [10 July 1977].

24. Robert Cushman. 'Loose lady in the dock'. Review. *Observer*. 10 July 1977. p. 26; Sheridan Morley. 'The Master Builder.' Review. *Punch*. 13 July 1977. p. 85.

25. John Barber. 'Profound study of woman in torment'. Review. *Daily Telegraph*. 5 July 1977.

26. *Cause Célèbre*. Dir. John Gorrie. (ITV, 1987). Network DVD, 2010.

27. Bartlett, *op. cit.*

28. Nicholas de Jongh. *Evening Standard*. 11 February 1998. All reviews of this production taken from *Theatre Record*, 18.3 (2 March), pp. 140–146.

29. Georgina Brown. *Mail on Sunday*. 15 February 1998; Michael Billington. *The Guardian*. 11 February 1998.

30. Bartlett, *op. cit.*

31. Levin, *op. cit.*

32. Havers, Shankland and Barrett, *op. cit.*, p. 219.

33. 'Cause to applaud'. *Daily Telegraph*. 2 December 1977.

CAUSE CÉLÈBRE

Cause Célèbre was first performed at Her Majesty's Theatre, London, on 4 July 1977, presented by John Gale. The cast was as follows:

ALMA RATTENBURY	Glynis Johns
FRANCIS RATTENBURY	Anthony Pedley
CHRISTOPHER	Matthew Ryan / Douglas Melbourne
IRENE RIGGS	Sheila Grant
GEORGE WOOD	Neil Daglish
EDITH DAVENPORT	Helen Lindsay
JOHN DAVENPORT	Jeremy Hawk
TONY DAVENPORT	Adam Richardson
STELLA MORRISON	Angela Browne
RANDOLPH BROWNE	Kevin Hart
JUDGE	Patrick Barr
O'CONNOR	Kenneth Griffith
CROOM-JOHNSON	Bernard Archard
CASSWELL	Darryl Forbes-Dawson
MONTAGU	Philip Bowen
CLERK OF THE COURT	David Glover
JOAN WEBSTER	Peggy Aitchison
SERGEANT BAGWELL	Anthony Pedley
PORTER	Anthony Howard
WARDER	David Masterman
CORONER	David Glover
Director	Robin Midgley
Designer	Adrian Vaux

THE OLD VIC

Cause Célèbre was performed as part of the Rattigan Centenary celebrations at The Old Vic, London, from 17 March–11 June 2011. The cast (in order of appearance) was as follows:

ALMA RATTENBURY	Anne-Marie Duff
EDITH DAVENPORT	Niamh Cusack
STELLA MORRISON	Lucy Robinson
JOHN DAVENPORT	Simon Chandler
TONY DAVENPORT	Freddie Fox
PORTER	Tristram Wymark
GEORGE WOOD	Tommy McDonnell
IRENE RIGGS	Jenny Galloway
FRANCIS RATTENBURY	Timothy Carlton
CHRISTOPHER	Oliver Coopersmith
RANDOLPH BROWNE	Rory Fleck-Byrne
JOAN WEBSTER	Lucy Black
O'CONNOR	Nicholas Jones
MONTAGU	Rory Fleck-Byrne
CASSWELL	Richard Teverson
WARDER	Sarah Waddell
CLERK OF THE COURT	Tristan Shepherd
JUDGE	Patrick Godfrey
CROOM-JOHNSON	Richard Clifford
SERGEANT BAGWELL	Michael Webber
CORONER	Tristram Wymark

Director	Thea Sharrock
Designer	Hildegard Bechtler
Lighting	Bruno Poet
Music	Adrian Johnston
Sound	Ian Dickinson for Autograph
Casting	Sarah Bird

Characters

ALMA RATTENBURY
FRANCIS RATTENBURY
CHRISTOPHER
IRENE RIGGS
GEORGE WOOD
EDITH DAVENPORT
JOHN DAVENPORT
TONY DAVENPORT
STELLA MORRISON
RANDOLPH BROWNE
JUDGE
O'CONNOR
CROOM-JOHNSON
CASSWELL
MONTAGU
CLERK OF THE COURT
JOAN WEBSTER
POLICE SERGEANT BAGWELL
PORTER
WARDER
CORONER

The action of the play takes place in Bournemouth and London in 1934 and 1935.

This play was inspired by the facts of a well-known case, but the characters attributed to the individuals represented are based on the author's imagination, and are not necessarily factual.

ACT ONE

The stage represents at various times Court Number One at the Old Bailey and other parts of the Central Criminal Court in London, a villa at Bournemouth, the drawing room of a flat in Kensington and other places. Changes of scene are effected mainly by lighting, the curtain falling only at the end of each of the two acts.

Lights on ALMA RATTENBURY *and* MRS EDITH DAVENPORT. *After a moment, light comes up very dimly on the* CLERK OF THE COURT.

CLERK OF THE COURT. Alma Victoria Rattenbury, you are charged with the murder of Francis Mawson Rattenbury on March the twenty-eighth, 1935. Are you guilty or not guilty?

ALMA (*almost inaudibly*). Not guilty.

The lights change as the CLERK OF THE COURT *turns towards* MRS DAVENPORT.

CLERK OF THE COURT. Edith Amelia Davenport, take the book in your right hand and read what is on this card.

The light on the CLERK OF THE COURT *slowly fades out.*

MRS DAVENPORT. I do solemnly swear by Almighty God that I will well and truly try the issues joined between our Sovereign Lord the King and the prisoners at the bar and will give a true verdict according to the evidence.

The spots fade out on ALMA *and* MRS DAVENPORT.

MRS DAVENPORT *and* STELLA MORRISON *in the sitting room of the flat in Kensington.* STELLA *is* MRS DAVENPORT*'s sister, a year or two younger.*

STELLA. A jury summons! – My dear, how too frightful. Let's see.

MRS DAVENPORT *hands her the official letter.*

(*Reading.*) '... present yourself at the... jury service... for fifteen days... and fail not at your peril' – indeed!

MRS DAVENPORT (*smiling*). Yes, rather scaring, that. Peril of what, d'you think? Hard labour, or the stocks, or just a ducking?

STELLA. Whopping great fine, I should think. Might almost be worth paying it. I'll get Henry to cough up the necessary if you like.

MRS DAVENPORT (*taking back the letter*). Certainly not. I'm quite looking forward to it, as it happens.

STELLA. What, a whole fortnight?

MRS DAVENPORT. Well, I've got the time these days, and who knows, I might do a bit of good for some old soul who's snitched a pair of silk stockings from Barkers.

STELLA. More likely to be indecent exposure.

MRS DAVENPORT. Oh, they wouldn't have women on those juries, would they?

STELLA. My dear, they have women on everything these days.

MRS DAVENPORT. Well, if it is that, I'll just have to face it like – well, like a man, I suppose. But I'm not going on that date – I'm not going to mess up Tony's Christmas hols. I'll ask for a postponement to May, that should be safe.

STELLA. Is he enjoying himself in Cannes?

MRS DAVENPORT. Tony? He says so in his postcards, but I expect they're written under John's supervision. Thank heavens it's the last time.

STELLA. You're still determined on the divorce?

MRS DAVENPORT. Yes. Quite.

STELLA. Well, you know what I think.

MRS DAVENPORT. A separation doesn't give me custody.

STELLA. You won't get *complete* custody.

MRS DAVENPORT. Oh yes I will. John won't defend it. He's too scared of his undersecretary. It'll all be fixed out of court. If he does defend it, I'll win.

STELLA. There was only that one woman, wasn't there?

MRS DAVENPORT. Oh no. In the five years before we separated I've found out now there were at least two others. And now there's this dreadful woman.

STELLA. Still, four in five years? That doesn't really make him Bluebeard, you know. In fact, for most husbands with unwilling wives I'd say it was about par for the course.

MRS DAVENPORT. Are you trying to make it my fault again?

STELLA. Well, he was only about forty, wasn't he, when you started having headaches? That *is* a bit young, darling, for a husband to find himself in the spare room.

MRS DAVENPORT. I couldn't go on, Stella. I told you. I never did care much for that side of things, as you know, and as he got older he got more and more demanding.

STELLA. That's one thing I could never say about Henry –

MRS DAVENPORT. He used to say that my reluctance made him want it more. Now, you can't say that's normal, Stella.

STELLA. I suppose not – I just wonder if it would work with Henry… How does Tony feel about it all? He always seemed to be quite fond of his father.

MRS DAVENPORT. Well, he was. Of course, now that I've told him the truth – not all of it, of course, just enough – he's beginning to see things my way. Unless he's been led astray these last two weeks. I wouldn't put anything past that man. I really hate him.

Fade out.

DAVENPORT. There should be a car waiting to pick me up. The name's Davenport – would you put that one down there and come back for the other?

PORTER. Very good, sir! (*Goes.*)

DAVENPORT. Well, Tony, I'm afraid this is goodbye. You had better take the airport bus to Victoria Air Terminus, and get a taxi to Kensington from there… I'm going straight to the Home Office, so –

TONY (*quickly*). I understand. (*Pause*.) Dad, I will be seeing you again, won't I?

DAVENPORT. Well, certainly in court.

TONY. I meant after that?

DAVENPORT. I'm afraid that depends on your mother.

TONY. I see. Can I ask one thing?

DAVENPORT. Yes.

TONY. Mum always talks to me – well, sometimes talks to me about *that* woman, et cetera, et cetera!

DAVENPORT. Yes.

TONY. Well – there isn't any *that* woman, is there? I mean, I've been with you two weeks, and I'm not half-witted…

DAVENPORT. No, you're not.

TONY. You still love Mum, don't you?

DAVENPORT. Yes, I do.

TONY. Dad – is there any *that* woman?

Pause.

PORTER. I've found your car, sir; do you want the other one in the boot?

DAVENPORT. No, my son is travelling by the bus, so –

PORTER. Yes, sir. I'll get him a place.

TONY. Thank you.

DAVENPORT. I'll do the VIP. Well, goodbye, Tony.

TONY. Thank you for a marvellous time.

DAVENPORT. A bit dull, I'm afraid.

TONY. Not Cannes. That was smashing.

DAVENPORT. You didn't like Paris?

TONY. Well, don't think I'm ungrateful, Dad, but you did promise to take me a – to a – you know – that 'House of All Nations' –

DAVENPORT. Tony, I did remember that. It's just that – well, you have to take a passport, you see.

TONY. A passport to a brothel?

DAVENPORT. They're very strict about underage.

TONY (*despairing*). Oh, Dad! Even in France? I'll have to try – Turkey or somewhere.

DAVENPORT (*laughing*). Why Turkey? Why not here – Jermyn Street?

TONY. I'd thought of that, only I'm a bit – well –

DAVENPORT. I'm not serious. At least, not yet. I should give it another year or two, I think, old chap, don't you?

TONY. But Dad, I'm seventeen!

DAVENPORT. Yes, but that's still a bit young, don't you think? My first wasn't till I was twenty. But still, when you do go, for God's sake, take precautions, won't you?

TONY. What – ?

PORTER. I've got your place, sir.

DAVENPORT. Thank you. (*Gives him half a crown.*)

PORTER. Thank you, sir. (*Goes.*)

DAVENPORT. Well –

TONY. Dad, what shall I tell Mum – about *that* woman?

DAVENPORT. Tell her you didn't meet her, but I was always talking to her on the telephone. It's a question of her pride. Off you go, Tony.

GEORGE WOOD *crosses the stage to stand outside the* RATTENBURYS' *house, taking off his bicycle clips.*

The lights come up to show the hall, sitting room, stairs.
IRENE RIGGS, *maid and companion to* ALMA – *dressed
more as companion than maid – is entering the tiny hall.*

IRENE. Yes? What is it?

WOOD. I've come about the advert.

IRENE. You're too old.

WOOD. It says 'fourteen to eighteen'.

IRENE. I know what it says. I wrote it myself. You're too old.

WOOD. I'm seventeen.

IRENE. You're still not what we're wanting. Sorry.

ALMA (*calling from upstairs*). Who is it, Irene?

IRENE (*calling back*). A boy about the advert. He's wrong.

ALMA (*calling*). Why?

IRENE (*calling*). He's too old.

WOOD (*making voice heard aloft*). I'm not. I'm only seventeen.

IRENE (*calling*). But he looks much older.

ALMA (*after a pause, calling*). I'll come down.

IRENE (*calling*). I was sending him away.

ALMA (*decisively*). Keep him.

IRENE (*annoyed, to* WOOD). You'd better come in. (*Clicking
her tongue.*) You're not the type at all.

ALMA *has meanwhile swung her legs off the bed.*

ALMA (*calling*). I'll just slip into something. I won't be a mo.

*Pulls out a pair of day pyjamas – of a fairly hectic design
and colour – from the wardrobe.*

Downstairs, WOOD *has come in and is waiting uncertainly
in the hall, twisting his homburg hat.*

(*Calling.*) Tell him to go into the lounge, Irene, and make
himself comfortable.

IRENE (*nodding towards the sitting room*). You heard her.

WOOD (*on his way in*). You the maid?

IRENE. Companion.

WOOD. You don't like me, do you?

IRENE. I've nothing against you. You're just not the type, that's all.

WOOD. That'll be for her to say, won't it?

He nods upstairs. IRENE *regards him coldly.*

IRENE (*at length*). Yes, it will.

She goes down the passage and disappears. WOOD *looks round the sitting room and perches on a chair. Upstairs* ALMA *has finished her dressing and is applying lipstick, then patting her hair into place.* WOOD *gets up and goes to a small piano, on the stand of which is a piece of sheet music left open. He examines it.* ALMA *comes rapidly down the stairs in slippered feet and surprises him as she comes in. He starts guiltily away from the piano.*

WOOD. Sorry.

ALMA (*laughing*). That's quite all right. I don't mind anyone reading my music.

WOOD. Oh, I don't read music. Did you say *your* music?

ALMA. Look at the front.

WOOD (*awed*). That's a picture of you.

ALMA. Taken a long time ago, I'm afraid. It's twelve years old, that photograph.

WOOD. 'Dark-Haired Marie' by Lozanne. Is that you – Miss Lozanne?

ALMA. Oh no – that's just my pen-name. (*Seeing* WOOD's *bewilderment.*) It's just the name I put on my songs. My real name's Alma. What's yours?

WOOD. Wood.

ALMA. Christian name?

WOOD. Perce. Percy, really. My dad calls me Perce – so Perce.

ALMA. What does your dad do for a living?

WOOD. He's a builder, laid off. I work for him when he's got work – but there's not much of that about these days.

ALMA. Oh, I know. It's terrible, this slump. I can't sell a song these days – for love nor money.

WOOD. Do you do this for a living, miss?

ALMA. Oh no. I don't have to, thank heavens, or I'd be on the dole. Mind you, they do get done sometimes. That song, for instance, that was done only a year ago, on the BBC. A baritone sang it.

WOOD (*eagerly*). The Whispering Baritone?

ALMA. No. Just a baritone. Let me take your cap.

WOOD. Thank you, miss.

She takes it from him and puts it on the piano.

ALMA. By the way, it's 'Mrs'. Mrs three times over, as it happens –

WOOD. Cor. Divorced?

ALMA (*gaily*). Yes, once, the other one died and now seven years gone with old Ratz – Mr Rattenbury, my present one. I'm giving things away, aren't I? I started very young. I've a boy of thirteen. Almost as old as you.

She laughs. He smiles politely.

Yes, well… I suppose it's working on building sites that's made you so – developed.

WOOD. I bike a lot too.

ALMA. Yes. That does do wonders for the physique. You look quite what I would call – full-grown.

Pause. WOOD *has at last dimly realised the nature of his future mistress's interest in him.*

WOOD. Your – Irene – thought I was too full-grown.

ALMA. Yes. Well, you see we concocted that advertisement together, and what *she* had in mind was – well – a rather smaller kind of boy. You'd be under her, really, not me… Well, I'd better tell you what the wages are. It's one of the reasons we wanted a little boy. I'm afraid my husband will only go to a pound a week.

WOOD. Living in?

ALMA. No, I'm afraid not. We haven't room, really. There's only one other room besides Irene's, you see, and my two boys – I've another little one, only six – well, they're in there, during school holidays that is. Of course, if you'd been a little boy like I meant in the advert, you *could* have slept in with them – I mean, if you'd been a really *little* boy – but being as you are, and me and Irene slipping about upstairs with next to nothing on – well, it would be rather awkward, wouldn't it?… (*Rather breathlessly.*) No, I'm afraid living in's quite out of the question.

WOOD. I was only asking. Where does old Ratz sleep?

ALMA. Oh, you mustn't call him Ratz. You must call him Mr Rattenbury, like Irene.

WOOD. Yes. Where does he sleep?

Pause.

ALMA. Inquisitive, aren't you? That's all right. I like an enquiring nature. Mr Rattenbury sleeps through there.

She points to the door off the sitting room.

He can't do the stairs any more.

Pause.

WOOD. I see.

Pause.

ALMA (*lightly*). Well, is it a go, or isn't it?

WOOD. A quid isn't much.

ALMA. Well, I could slip you a few bob on the side – expenses, you know. Only Ratz – Mr Rattenbury mustn't know. He's a little strict about money. Do you live close?

WOOD. Other side of Bournemouth. About half hour on my bike. You wouldn't like to say how many bob?

ALMA (*patting his arm*). You must ask when you need it.

WOOD. Okay.

ALMA. Well, I'm glad that's settled. Why don't we have a little drinkie on it?

WOOD. I'm afraid I don't drink.

ALMA. I expect that's just what you tell all your employers. Gin and it?

WOOD. I don't know what that is.

ALMA. Fancy anyone not knowing what a 'gin and it' is!

She is busy pouring herself a drink.

…Won't you just try a sip, just to seal our little arrangement?

WOOD. If you insist.

ALMA. Oh, I don't *insist*. I never insist. But just this once – There has to be a first time for everything, doesn't there?

WOOD. Yes.

ALMA. A little of what you fancy's my motto, and a very good one too. This is a lovely world we're in, and we were put into it to enjoy it. Don't you agree?

She hands him the drink.

WOOD. I might. I don't think my dad would. He's religious.

ALMA. Well, our dear Lord didn't say we mustn't have fun, did He? He turned water into wine, not wine into water. Just tell that to your dad next time he gets narky. And He said we must love each other, and I think we should.

Raising her glass.

Well, Perce – no, I can't call you Perce. Or Percy. Have you got a middle name?

WOOD. George.

ALMA. That's nice. I'm going to call you that. (*Raising her glass again.*) George.

WOOD (*raising his*). Mrs Rattenbury.

ALMA. Alma… Not just now – always…

WOOD. Alma.

ALMA. George!

They drink. WOOD *makes a face.* ALMA *laughs and takes the glass away from him.*

I'm not letting you have any more. I'm not having anyone say I'm leading you astray.

She drinks WOOD*'s drink in a single gulp.*

– Just like water to me. Do you know what Alma means in Latin? A professor told me once, it means 'life-giving', 'bountiful'. In olden times they used it about goddesses, like Venus.

Sipping her drink.

Well, I'm not Venus, God knows – but apparently it also means 'kind and comforting', and that I am, George, though I say it who shouldn't –

FRANCIS RATTENBURY *comes into the hall.*

Here's Ratz. I'd better warn you. You have to shout.

She opens the sitting-room door. RATTENBURY *immediately glances at* WOOD. *Deaf he may be, but certainly not blind.* ALMA *kisses him.*

(*Loudly.*) Had a nice walkie?

RATTENBURY. There was an east wind. You should have told me.

ALMA. Poor thing, did you get chilled?

RATTENBURY. Blasted to buggery.

Paying no attention to WOOD, *he sits down in what is evidently his usual armchair – significantly one that has its back to a pair of French windows.*

Get me a whisky, would you?

ALMA. It's a bit early for your whisky, isn't it?

She begins to get him a drink.

RATTENBURY. It's a bit early for your gin.

ALMA. I only meant you don't usually have whisky in the mornings.

RATTENBURY. I don't usually get blasted to buggery in the morning.

Showing her a paper.

Shares are down again.

ALMA. Oh dear. You're probably wondering who the stranger is.

RATTENBURY. No, I wasn't, but who is he?

ALMA. His name is George Wood, and he's the new help.

RATTENBURY (*after a moody sip*). Irene said 'a boy'.

ALMA. Well, he *is* a boy. He's only seventeen.

RATTENBURY. Hm.

He stares at WOOD *without overmuch interest.*

Has he any references?

WOOD. No, sir. I've never done this kind of work before.

RATTENBURY. What?

ALMA (*putting her hand on his shoulder*). Don't worry, dear. We had a nice long interview. I'll vouch for him.

RATTENBURY *looks up at her. He grunts acquiescence and hands her his glass.*

That one went down pretty fast.

RATTENBURY. Not as fast as my shares.

As ALMA *passes* WOOD.

Does he drive?

WOOD (*loudly*). Yes, sir. I've got a licence.

ALMA (*coming back with the whisky*). Well, isn't that marvellous! (*To* RATTENBURY, *loudly*.) Isn't that handy, dear? We've got ourselves a chauffeur.

RATTENBURY. No uniform.

ALMA (*loudly*). No, of course not. (*To* WOOD, *quietly*.) Well, perhaps a cap and a smart mackintosh. You'd look nice in a cap.

RATTENBURY. What are you saying?

ALMA. I was explaining 'no uniform', dear. (*To* WOOD.) Better go now. (*Loudly, to* RATTENBURY.) I'm just showing the new help to the front door. (*To* WOOD.) Come on. (*To* RATTENBURY.) Back in a jiffy.

She and WOOD *go.*

– Well, that's settled, thank goodness. It's lovely about your driving. Go and buy yourself a cap. (*She fishes in her bag.*) Here's fifteen shillings. Will that be enough?

WOOD. Should be.

CHRISTOPHER *comes in, wearing his Scout's uniform.*

CHRISTOPHER. Mummy, there's a smashing bike outside, with low handlebars. (*Seeing* WOOD.) Oh, is it yours, sir?

WOOD. Yes. A Raleigh.

CHRISTOPHER. I was going to ask if I could ride it.

WOOD. Afraid I'm just going.

ALMA. But he's coming back tomorrow – and every day afterwards. He's going to be one of the family.

CHRISTOPHER. Oh, good.

ALMA. I'm sure if you ask him nicely he'll let you ride it.

WOOD. You bet.

CHRISTOPHER. Oh, thanks awfully, sir. Mummy, when's lunch?

ALMA. Quite soon, darling.

CHRISTOPHER (*calling and running off*). Irene!

CHRISTOPHER *disappears up the stairs.*

ALMA. Sweet, isn't he? (*Sincerely.*) I really am very blessed with my children.

WOOD (*in awe*). He called me 'sir'.

ALMA. What? (*Misunderstanding.*) Oh, they teach him that at his school. Don't worry. He'll soon be calling you George.

WOOD. I'd rather he went on calling me 'sir'.

ALMA. I'll see he does then.

IRENE *appears from the shadows.*

(*Hastily to* WOOD.) Goodbye then. I'll see you tomorrow.

WOOD. What time?

ALMA. What time, Irene?

Pause.

IRENE (*at length, gloomily*). Seven. Not a second later.

ALMA. Can you manage seven?

WOOD. Easy… Be seeing you.

He goes out. ALMA, *left alone with* IRENE, *is uneasy under her steady stare.*

IRENE (*at length*). You'll have my notice at the end of the week.

ALMA *laughs and embraces her fondly.*

ALMA. Yes, darling, I'm sure I will.

IRENE. I'm serious.

ALMA. You always are. He can drive, Irene, which is more than any of your little teenies could have done.

IRENE. Yes. There's something else he can do that my little teenies couldn't.

ALMA. Irene...

IRENE. Anyway, you owe me four weeks' wages.

ALMA. Six pounds?

She looks in her bag.

Oh dear. And there's Christopher's new cricket bat. (*Nodding towards the sitting room.*) He's in a bad mood... still, he's got a couple of whiskies inside him. Think of something for me –

IRENE. I don't know.

ALMA. Pray for me.

IRENE. Yes.

She goes into the sitting room. IRENE *exits.*

ALMA *goes up to* RATTENBURY.

ALMA (*to* RATTENBURY, *brightly*). Well, Ratz, darling. Let me get you another little drinkie. There's time for one before lunch.

She takes his now empty glass to refill it.

(*Loudly.*) I've been showing George the car.

RATTENBURY. Who's George?

ALMA. Our new chauffeur, darling... (*Brings the drink to him.*) He says it's in spanking condition, except just for one little thing – (*Sits down, smiling lovingly.*) It needs a new carburettor. He says if we don't have one the car might seize up altogether, and that would mean a new car, darling.

RATTENBURY. Well, we'll have to walk then, won't we?

ALMA (*laughing merrily*). Oh, you are a scream...

RATTENBURY (*chokes on his drink*). This is too strong.

ALMA *takes the glass and puts more water in it.*

ALMA. Now, after lunch we'll get your chequebook out and write out a cheque.

RATTENBURY. I won't sign it.

She comes back with the drink, and lays her hand lovingly on his head.

ALMA. Oh yes you will, dear. You're far too kind and loving a husband not to. (*Kisses the top of his head.*) Oh, I do love my darling Ratz.

The lights fade.

TONY. Mum! Listen to this – Did you know Mrs Rattenbury and Wood battered old Rattenbury on the head so hard they completely smashed his skull.

MRS DAVENPORT. What? Oh, you're reading about that awful murder. A few years ago, a case like that wouldn't even have been mentioned in *The Times*... be a darling...

TONY. That's what makes it so funny, it happening in Bournemouth.

MRS DAVENPORT. I don't see that that's funny.

TONY. On Aunt Stella's doorstep... And ours, when we get that house. I wonder what their defence will be. Wood's statement says he was doped on cocaine, and the police say Mrs Rattenbury was as drunk as a fly.

MRS DAVENPORT. Tony, I don't want you to talk about it. And you shouldn't be reading it. Haven't you your homework to do?

TONY. Finished. Mum, could I ask you a question?

MRS DAVENPORT. Of course.

TONY. If you'd found out before you started the divorce that there wasn't another woman at all with Dad, would it have made any difference?

Pause.

MRS DAVENPORT. But there is another woman.

TONY. No, there isn't. I'm sure there isn't. And I honestly think he'd come back, if you asked him.

MRS DAVENPORT. On his terms...

TONY. I don't know what they are.

MRS DAVENPORT. I can't explain it to you, darling. You're far too young to understand...

TONY (*with unexpected vehemence*). That isn't true! Please believe me – I understand much more than you know.

Pause.

MRS DAVENPORT. ... Is Randolph coming here, or are you going to him?

TONY. He's coming here.

MRS DAVENPORT (*takes a note from her handbag*). Is ten shillings enough?

TONY. Oh, plenty.

MRS DAVENPORT. And for the cinema too?

TONY. It's only The Kensington.

MRS DAVENPORT (*sharply*). What's the film?

TONY. I don't remember the title. It's got Irene Dunne –

MRS DAVENPORT (*relieved*). That should be very nice. You haven't told me yet how you like my new dress.

TONY. Spiffing. Who are you out to impress?

MRS DAVENPORT. Stella's coming to take me to have dinner with General and Lady Whitworth.

TONY. Oh yes. And they're important because of the new house, or something.

MRS DAVENPORT. He's Chairman of the Bournemouth Country Club, which owns the whole estate – He's a terrible old snob, according to Stella, so I expect it'll be an excruciating evening. A lot of small talk about gout and cricket, and trouble with the undergardeners.

TONY. Is it worth it?

MRS DAVENPORT. Oh yes, darling, it's a lovely little house – quite perfect for just the two of us, so I'll have to be a good girl and say all the right things. They're determined only to let in 'a certain class of person'!

TONY. Not Mrs Rattenbury! (*Laughs*). Oops, sorry.

MRS DAVENPORT *smiles*.

You don't have to worry, Mum, I'm sure you'll manage your grapefruit perfectly.

MRS DAVENPORT. And not eat peas with a knife?

TONY. Or tell any of those filthy stories of yours.

He laughs.

MRS DAVENPORT (*embracing him*). You're a naughty boy. Your hair needs cutting.

TONY. Tomorrow.

There is a ring at the front door.

MRS DAVENPORT. Just stay and say hullo, and then leave us alone for a moment, will you? (*Calling off*.) Hello, Stella, did you come by car?

She goes out. We hear the sound of greeting in the hall. TONY fishes out the discarded copy of the Evening News, *folds it up and puts it into his breast pocket.*

STELLA comes in, also wearing evening dress but, because she is rich, probably a real Chanel rather than a fake Molyneux.

STELLA (*as she comes in*). No, I sent the Rolls on ahead and had Phillips pick me up off the train. It wasn't the Belle, of course, but it had a perfectly good Pullman – hullo Tony.

TONY. Hullo, Aunt Stella.

He allows himself to be kissed.

STELLA. You get handsomer every time I see you. (*To* MRS DAVENPORT.) Any girls in his life yet?

MRS DAVENPORT. Oh yes… Happily they all live in Hollywood.

STELLA (*to* TONY). Wouldn't nearer be better?

MRS DAVENPORT (*sharply*). He's too young for girls.

STELLA. Darling, I wasn't being serious. My dear, what about this murder case!

TONY. Did you ever meet her, Aunt Stella?

STELLA. Mrs Rattenbury? Oh no. But the awful thing is I suppose one could have. Your Uncle Henry, of course, is going around boasting he *did* meet her – at a cocktail party somewhere – and she sang one of her songs. But you know what a liar he is. By next week he'll have had an affair with her –

TONY. Which wasn't too difficult, I gather.

STELLA. Difficult for Henry – even with Mrs Rattenbury. I said to him – 'You'd better be careful, dear. You don't know what the gardener's boy and I get up to when you're up at the Stock Exchange. We might swing a mallet on you any time – '

TONY (*excitedly*). Do you think they both swung together, or took it in turns? I mean, did Wood hit the old boy first and then she finished him off – or –

STELLA. Oh, they both swung together, of course – like two Etonians.

(*Singing.*) 'And we'll both swing together, and swear by the best of – ' what? Not 'schools' – 'pools' would do. I gather from the Commissioner there was a pool of blood all over the floor, inches deep – and she was dancing the black bottom in it.

TONY. No, really?

STELLA. Stark naked, my dear, and trying to kiss all the policemen – and shouting out, 'I did it, I did it – I bumped him off!'

MRS DAVENPORT (*violently*). Will you please stop!

STELLA *looks at her uneasily. She knows her sister's temperament.*

TONY. Mum's very shocked by it all.

STELLA. Well, of course she is. Of course we all are. (*To her sister.*) But with a thing as appalling as this – and in the heart of Bournemouth too – the only thing one can do is to make a joke of it. If one starts trying to think of it seriously, one would go mad. I mean, it being with a servant! To me, that's the real horror.

MRS DAVENPORT. Tony, go to your room.

TONY. Yes, Mum. (*Kisses* STELLA.) Goodbye, Aunt Stella.

MRS DAVENPORT. Goodnight, darling.

TONY *kisses her.*

I'll try not to disgrace you with the General.

TONY. You'll be a smashing success, I know. (*Goes.*)

MRS DAVENPORT. To me the real horror is the boy's age – exactly the same age as Tony –

STELLA. When he met her perhaps. Now he's a year older. Eighteen. Old enough to hang.

MRS DAVENPORT. Oh God! The law's unjust. It's the woman who should hang.

STELLA. Oh, she will. No doubt of that, thank heavens. But after all, the boy did kill his employer. He really shouldn't get away with that.

MRS DAVENPORT (*violently*). I don't know. I only know *she* ought to be lynched!

STELLA. Well, she might be. You should hear what they're saying about her in Bournemouth –

MRS DAVENPORT. I suppose I'm being silly but whenever I think about that horrible case, I think about Tony.

STELLA. Yes. I'm afraid you are being rather silly, darling. I doubt if Tony's going to commit murder for a middle-aged

nympho-dipso-songwriter. There can't be many in
Bournemouth.

MRS DAVENPORT (*darkly*). There was a married woman at
Dieppe last Christmas, well over thirty, who had an eye on
him. French too.

STELLA. Was Tony interested?

MRS DAVENPORT. I didn't give him a chance to be. I changed
hotels.

STELLA. Yes. You would. There are worse ways for a boy to
start than with a married woman who knows how to take the
right precautions – coupled with a bit of French élan.

MRS DAVENPORT. Stella!

There is a ring at the front door.

Just a moment –

She goes out. We hear her voice.

(*Off.*) Oh, hullo, Randolph.

BROWNE (*off*). Hullo, Mrs Davenport.

MRS DAVENPORT (*off*). Tony's in his bedroom. You know
where that is.

BROWNE (*off*). Yes. Thank you.

She comes back.

Tony's best pal at Westminster. Randolph Browne. A
bishop's son – and a very good friend for him…

STELLA. Well, shall we go?

MRS DAVENPORT. There's something I want to ask you.
Should I mention tonight about John and…?

STELLA. Not the bed part –

MRS DAVENPORT. Really! As if I would –

STELLA. …Well, don't mention the word 'divorce' tonight.
Leave it to me. When's the decree absolute?

MRS DAVENPORT. Not for another couple of months.

STELLA. Well, I hope it's not in the *Bournemouth Echo* –

MRS DAVENPORT. Stella – after all, I am the innocent party.

STELLA. My dear, in Bournemouth *nobody* in a divorce is ever the innocent party.

MRS DAVENPORT. Well, let them see me as a glamorous divorcée then.

STELLA (*as she goes*). Frankly, darling, I don't think that's very likely either.

MRS DAVENPORT. It's all clear, Tony.

TONY (*off*). Thank you. Goodbye.

Fade on the sitting room as they go out, and fade up on the bedroom, where RANDOLPH BROWNE, *bespectacled and studious, sits, deep in the* Evening Standard. *Beside him sits* TONY, *deep in his rescued* Evening News. *There is a pause.*

BROWNE (*at length*). Have you got to the orgy in the Royal Palace Hotel?

TONY. I wonder how many times they did it all together…

BROWNE. From the time he went to live in the house – which was – it's here somewhere – Yes – 'Congress first took place a month after he was employed – '

TONY. 'Congress'?

BROWNE. Legal for 'it'.

TONY. What about the Congress of Anglican Bishops? (*As he makes his calculation*.) Assuming twice a night for…

BROWNE. Why only twice a night? He wasn't in training for anything.

TONY. You mean *you* could have made it more?

BROWNE. Double – easily.

TONY. Bollocks – Here it is. At twice a night until the murder, three hundred and fourteen times!

BROWNE. You know, when they open that trapdoor he'll probably float upwards, not drop downwards.

TONY. I'm not being funny, Browne. I really do almost envy him...

BROWNE. Mind you, three hundred and fourteen times – That's nothing in a lifetime, and for him it will be a lifetime, poor sod. I hope to put up a million before I die.

TONY. Not a hope. You'll never get enough girls.

BROWNE. You only need one.

TONY. When you're eighty it'll probably still be Jones Minor.

BROWNE. You're out of date.

TONY. Who is it now?

BROWNE. Shuttleworth.

TONY. I don't know him.

BROWNE. He's in the choir.

TONY. God, you are disgusting! Randy by name, and randy by nature.

BROWNE. That's right. Anyway, a chap's got to do something, hasn't he? Or else he'd go raving mad.

Pause.

TONY. It's hell, isn't it?

BROWNE. Oh, I don't know. It'll do till something better comes along.

TONY. But when will that be? God, it's frustrating. To be seventeen is hell... I mean, seventeen and English and upper class and living in this century is hell... It wasn't always like that. Romeo was only seventeen, Juliet only thirteen.

BROWNE. And a ripe mess they made of things.

TONY. But no one in Shakespeare's time thought they were too *young*, did they? 'A boy of seventeen and a girl of thirteen? How too utterly disgusting, my dear!'

BROWNE. Your mother?

TONY *nods*.

Not a good imitation.

Doing his own imitation, evidently of his father.

'My dear Randolph, should you be troubled with impure thoughts, you will find a cold tub and a brisk trot will work wonders – '

TONY. The bishop?

BROWNE. Verbatim.

TONY. I wonder what our parents think we *do* between thirteen and twenty-one.

BROWNE. Solo, I should think, or else have cold tubs and brisk trots.

TONY. It's such damn humbug. Of course, they know we're safe – apart from Shuttleworths, which they don't like to think about. You should have heard my mother on this Mrs Rattenbury. The murder apart, my mother seems to think she's the monster of Glamis, just because she's twenty years older than Wood... And why not? Look at her. (*Slaps the paper.*) She's damned attractive.

BROWNE. Not bad at all.

TONY (*muttering*). Three hundred and fourteen times. My God, I've a good mind to – and with Mum out – How much money have you got?

BROWNE. 'Good mind to' what?

TONY. Try it. Tonight.

BROWNE. With Mrs Rattenbury?

TONY. No, idiot. 'It.'

BROWNE. Oh. (*Counting.*) Seventeen and threepence.

TONY. And I've got ten bob. What do you suppose we could get for one pound seven and threepence?

BROWNE. Both of us?

TONY. Don't you want to?

BROWNE. Not for – thirteen and sevenpence halfpenny, thank you.

TONY. Will you lend it to me then?

BROWNE. Are you serious?

TONY. Yes.

BROWNE. I know nothing about it.

He hands him fifteen shillings.

TONY. Why? What can happen to me? She can only say no. (*Goes to the door, and stops nervously.*) You won't come with me?

BROWNE. Davenport, you are speaking to the son of a bishop. When I do it it'll be Jermyn Street, and a fiver. I think I should warn you, my dear child, that it's not going to be Romeo and Juliet – or even Wood and Mrs Rattenbury...

The lights begin to fade.

TONY (*calling off*). Be out when Mum gets back.

BROWNE. I'm not staying here!

The lights now come up to illumine a small cell, at the moment empty. We hear the sound of a metal door being unlocked.

JOAN (*off*). In there.

ALMA comes on. As a remand prisoner she is allowed to wear her own clothes, and she has on a simple but smart dress. She is followed by a wardress (JOAN WEBSTER), a gruff-voiced, rather forbidding woman, younger than ALMA.

Wait.

She goes across the cell to another unseen door, which we hear opening. Then a murmur of voices. Finally, JOAN returns. ALMA meanwhile sits.

I didn't say you could sit.

ALMA. Sorry, dear.

She gets up.

JOAN. If the lawyers allow you to, that is their business. I have to obey prison regulations.

ALMA. Yes, of course. What's your name, dear?

JOAN. Wardress Webster.

ALMA. I mean your Christian name.

JOAN. We are not allowed to use first names.

ALMA. Phyllis did. And she used to call me Alma.

JOAN. Who is Phyllis?

ALMA. The other lady. The one that's gone on leave.

JOAN. Oh, Mrs Stringer. Well, she should not have.

ALMA. Oh, I'm sure it was quite wrong. But she was an awful dear, all the same. (*Laughs.*) She used to tell me about her little son, same age as my youngest – my little John.

No response from JOAN.

Poor little John… Oh well, he doesn't know yet. Christopher – that's my eldest – he does, of course. But in his letters he's quite cheerful.

No response from JOAN.

Of course, he doesn't quite understand…

Her voice trails off.

How long do you think my trial will last?

JOAN. I could not say, I'm sure.

ALMA. Mr Montagu – such a dear, Mr Montagu, and so good looking too – he says it'll last five days. What will I be allowed to wear?

JOAN. It will be your privilege to dress exactly as you please.

ALMA. Could I wear my pyjamas?

JOAN. I would think what you are currently wearing would be more suitable.

ALMA. Oh, I wasn't serious. Phyllis would have seen the joke. No, I mean, that's what they always write about. 'The female prisoner, wearing a fetching blue ensemble'... Well, they did at the Magistrates' Court, anyway. I just can't go on wearing a 'fetching blue ensemble' five days running. I mean, on the fifth day it'll stop 'fetching' and start carrying...

She laughs gaily. JOAN *does not crack a smile.*

(*After a pause.*) What made you become a wardress, dear? Did you think you were cut out for it?

JOAN. We are not allowed to answer personal questions.

ALMA. Aren't you? Phyllis always told me –

JOAN. Mrs Stringer may have had other ideas. I prefer to abide by the rules.

ALMA. Yes –

There is the sound of a metal door opening.

O'CONNOR (*off*). Thank you, Chief.

JOAN (*rapping out the order*). Prisoner Rattenbury, on your feet.

ALMA (*a shade plaintively*). I am on my feet.

O'CONNOR *and* MONTAGU *come in.*

O'CONNOR (*as they come in*). I don't know... quite frankly we'll have our work cut out, whoever we get. If we come up at the end of May, it'll probably be Humphreys. Just so long as it isn't Goddard!... All right, wardress, you may leave us.

JOAN. Sir.

She marches out.

O'CONNOR. Good morning.

ALMA. Good morning.

O'CONNOR. Sit down, please, Mrs Rattenbury.

ALMA. Oh, thank you –

She sits down. Both barristers sit at a table facing her.
O'CONNOR busily arranges papers in front of him.
MONTAGU, a young man, opens a packet of Player's
cigarettes and offers it to her.

MONTAGU. Mrs Rattenbury.

ALMA. – Player's. My favourites. Oh, Mr Montagu, you are a
duck.

He hands her the packet.

MONTAGU. Will those keep you for a time?

ALMA. Oh yes.

MONTAGU. Is there anything else I can get you that you need?

ALMA. Well, not really things that a man would know about,
kirby grips and things. Irene will see to those.

MONTAGU. She's still coming to see you?

ALMA. Oh yes. You can't keep her away.

O'CONNOR. Mrs Rattenbury, do you persist in saying that
your various statements to the police regarding the murder
are true?

ALMA. Well, I *can't* go back on them, can I?

O'CONNOR. You can very easily go back on them. In fact, Mrs
Rattenbury, to save your life – I repeat that – to save your
life, you must.

ALMA. Mr O'Connor. I'd like to say the things you want me to
say, I really would. But I can't.

O'CONNOR. Very well. Let me read to you some of the official
statements you made to the police. Late on the night of the
murder, after the body had been removed to hospital, you say
to Inspector Mills: 'I was playing cards with my husband
when he dared me to kill him as he wanted to die. I picked
up a mallet, and he said, "You have not the guts to do it." I
then hit him with the mallet.' Did you say that?… Mrs
Rattenbury, please pay attention.

ALMA. Yes. I'm sorry. What?

O'CONNOR. Did you say that to Inspector Mills?

ALMA. Yes.

O'CONNOR. You remember saying every word?

ALMA. Yes.

O'CONNOR. In spite of having consumed the best part of a bottle of whisky?

ALMA. My mind was perfectly clear.

O'CONNOR. 'Perfectly clear'? Half an hour before you signed that you were playing the gramophone full blast, dancing about the room half-dressed, and trying to kiss several of the policemen –

ALMA. Oh dear! Was I really? They didn't say that at the Magistrates' Court.

O'CONNOR. No, because it didn't suit their case. But they'll say it at the trial because it'll suit mine.

ALMA. Oh… Must you?… Dancing about half-naked, and –

She covers her face and shoulders.

– Oh dear! How could I have!

O'CONNOR. You mean you don't remember doing that?

ALMA. No. Nothing like that at all. Just a lot of noise and people there, and me trying to forget and – oh, how awful! Oh, I couldn't have –

O'CONNOR. This has come to you as a complete surprise.

ALMA. Oh yes –

O'CONNOR. And yet you remember *clearly every word* of a statement you made only half an hour later, when according to the police you had had even more to drink?… Mrs Rattenbury!

ALMA *looks up at him, realising she is caught.*

And you'll say that in court?

ALMA. I certainly will.

O'CONNOR. Right. Where did you find this mallet?

Pause.

ALMA. Lying about.

O'CONNOR. In the sitting room?

ALMA. No. It couldn't have been, could it? It must have been in the hall.

O'CONNOR. Did you know that Wood had borrowed it from his father earlier that evening?

ALMA. No.

O'CONNOR. What did you do with the mallet afterwards?

ALMA. I hid it.

O'CONNOR. Why?

ALMA *hesitates*.

If you were going to confess, why did you hide it?

ALMA. It looked so horrible.

O'CONNOR. More horrible than the body of your husband with his head caved in?

ALMA (*with a half-scream*). Don't –

O'CONNOR. I must. *Where* did you hide it, Mrs Rattenbury?

ALMA. I can't remember, even now.

O'CONNOR. Why should Wood know where the mallet was, and not you?

ALMA. He didn't know.

O'CONNOR. He did. On his arrest, two days after yours, he described to the police exactly where he had hidden it in the garden. And exactly there they found it – with his fingerprints all over it.

ALMA. Well, they would be. He'd carried it all the way from his father's.

O'CONNOR. And why weren't yours on it?

Pause.

ALMA. I wore gloves.

O'CONNOR. Where did you find the gloves?

ALMA. Oh, I have them upstairs. Lots of pairs.

Pause.

O'CONNOR. Your story then is this: your husband asks you to kill him. You agree. You go out into the hall to find a suitable implement, and find a gardener's mallet, borrowed that evening by Wood. You leave it there, go upstairs and choose a pair of gloves. You come downstairs, pick up the mallet in your gloved hands and hit your husband three times on the back of the head – the *back* of the head, Mrs Rattenbury, not the front –

ALMA. Don't – don't –

O'CONNOR. And kill him. You then hide the mallet somewhere in the garden, but you can't remember where, and presumably you put the gloves back in a drawer of your bedroom. You then ring up the police, to whom you give a full confession.

ALMA *is silent. She is trapped and knows it.*

Mrs Rattenbury, if I told that story in court, the jury's laughter would drown my voice.

ALMA (*indifferent*). Well, if they don't believe it, that's that.

O'CONNOR. No, it isn't quite that, Mrs Rattenbury. If I tell that story in court, do you know what the jury will believe, they will believe that it was Wood who killed your husband, with a mallet specially acquired for precisely that purpose, and that he did so with your knowledge and your consent, certainly under your influence, and very probably at your urging. That will make you both equally guilty of murder, and your efforts to shield Wood will have the effect of putting a noose around his neck just as surely as around your own.

ALMA. You're just trying to scare me. If I say I did it alone, how can they find *him* guilty?

O'CONNOR. They can and they will. Mrs Rattenbury, would you like to tell us the truth?

ALMA, *struggling to keep her composure, finds it hard to reply. But when she does her voice is firm and unwavering.*

ALMA. I've already told you, I killed Ratz alone and George had nothing to do with it.

Pause. O'CONNOR *stares at her steadily, then begins to put his papers together.*

O'CONNOR. Montagu – it seems there is nothing more.

MONTAGU. Mr O'Connor. Might I – ?

O'CONNOR. By all means.

He continues to gather his papers. MONTAGU *leans forward with a smile.*

MONTAGU. Mrs Rattenbury, we've come to know each other quite well in the last few weeks, haven't we?

ALMA. Oh yes, very well.

MONTAGU. During our talks, one of those things I've found out about you is that you're a very affectionate person. I mean, for instance, you told me how much you like that wardress –

ALMA. Phyllis? Oh yes. She's a dear.

MONTAGU. And Irene Riggs.

ALMA. I love Irene.

MONTAGU. Then you've told me often how fond you were of your husband.

ALMA. Old Ratz? (*Sincerely.*) Yes. He was a funny old thing in his way, but I *was* fond of him. Very fond of him, really.

MONTAGU (*gently*). Mrs Rattenbury, how can you possibly expect *me* – to believe that you deliberately hit him with a garden mallet with such force that his blood gushed out on the carpet –

ALMA. Stop…

MONTAGU. – at the first stroke, that you shattered his skull with the second –

ALMA (*jumping up*). Stop it, stop it!

MONTAGU. – opening up his head so that his brains were exposed –

ALMA (*screaming*). No, no, no! Stop it!

She puts her hands over her ears. MONTAGU *continues inexorably.*

MONTAGU. – that you changed the grip on the mallet and hit him on the right side of his head, opening up a gash just over the eye from which the blood spurted half across the room, and would have blinded him helplessly if he'd stayed alive –

ALMA, *hands to her ears, is now sobbing helplessly.*

– and that you coldly left him there in that chair to die, suffocating in his own blood – while you calmly hid the mallet in the garden, and the gloves upstairs.

Helpless with sobs, she has tried now to get away from him as far as she can, but he comes up to her.

How can you expect me to believe that you, of all people, did that to him?

Moaning, she makes no reply. With a brusque gesture he pulls her hands from her ears.

Above all, how can you go on loving and shielding the man who did?

She falls into a chair, sobbing. He puts his hand gently on her shoulder.

He joins O'CONNOR, *who has been watching the scene dispassionately, except for a faint annoyance that it was his junior and not himself that achieved the breakthrough. He presses a bell.*

O'CONNOR (*in what he plainly thinks is an inaudible murmur*). Yes. That was quite good work, Montagu.

JOAN *comes in.*

MONTAGU. We're going, wardress.

JOAN. Yes, sir. On your feet, Rattenbury.

MONTAGU. No, no. Let her sit for a moment.

JOAN (*understanding the reason*). Yes, sir.

MONTAGU. Please try and save your life, Mrs Rattenbury,
believe me, I think it's worth saving.

JOAN goes off with the two lawyers.

O'CONNOR (*off*). But it's just a matter of timing, you see. A
breakthrough of that kind is of little moment unless one can
follow it up at once. And that, of course – after you, my dear
fellow – you were quite unable to do.

*We hear a door clang, then JOAN comes back. ALMA's
tears have nearly stopped, but it is plain that her small
handkerchief has become a soggy ball. JOAN watches her
for a moment in silence, then reaches for the 'soggy ball' and
substitutes for it a massive but serviceable handkerchief of
her own.*

ALMA (*seated*). Ta.

*She wipes her eyes and face, offers the handkerchief back to
JOAN.*

JOAN. Keep it.

ALMA. Thank you, love. Thank you, Wardress Webster.

*She stuffs the vast napkin into her bag and stands up. JOAN
pushes her roughly back again. Then, after a lot of fumbling,
she produces a packet of cigarettes and proffers it.*

JOAN (*at length*). What is it?

ALMA. Nothing. They're trying to get me to say something and
I won't, that's all.

JOAN. They usually know best.

ALMA. Not in this case. In this case I know best. You see,
Wardress Webster –

JOAN. Joan –

ALMA. Well, you see, Joan, they both seemed to think just now that I didn't want to save my life – as if anyone in the world doesn't want to save their life – me above all others. I love life – I always have.

JOAN nods sympathetically.

It's just the cost, you see –

She could be speaking about the price of a length of crêpe de Chine. JOAN nods sympathetically, however, as if she understood. The lights fade.

The lights come up on the sitting room.

STELLA. Is anything the matter, Tony?

TONY. No, nothing!

STELLA. Nervous?

MRS DAVENPORT. Petrified.

STELLA. I heard on the wireless there's an enormous crowd already, and they're getting out mounted police for tomorrow. 'Fears for the female prisoner's safety' or something… I suppose you're sure you'll be in Court Number One?

MRS DAVENPORT. Yes. 'Fraid so.

STELLA. Have you got your speech ready?

MRS DAVENPORT. I know what I'm going to say. I can't judge this woman fairly and no power on earth can make me.

STELLA. Are you sure you wouldn't like a coffee?

MRS DAVENPORT. Oh, all right, yes.

STELLA. It's very sweet of you to have these qualms but if I were you I'd go in there, play noughts and crosses for four or five days, and then vote guilty with the eleven others.

She goes out.

MRS DAVENPORT. Tony, what's the matter with you?

TONY. Nothing.

Pause.

MRS DAVENPORT. I know what it is.

TONY (*startled*). What?

MRS DAVENPORT. You've written to Irene Dunne, and she hasn't answered.

TONY doesn't reply. MRS DAVENPORT gets up to go to the door.

TONY. Mum – I want to see Dad.

MRS DAVENPORT. You can't – without my permission.

TONY. I want your permission.

Pause.

MRS DAVENPORT. When?

TONY. Now. Tonight.

MRS DAVENPORT. Certainly not.

TONY. I have to see him. I have to. It's a matter of life and death –

MRS DAVENPORT. Don't be absurd.

TONY. I meant that literally, Mum. Life and death. What's more, whether I get your permission or not, I'm going to see him – now, if he's in. If he's not, I'll wait until he is.

Pause.

MRS DAVENPORT. What happened?

TONY. I can't tell you.

Pause.

MRS DAVENPORT. There's nothing you can't tell me. Whatever it is, Tony, you've got to tell me.

TONY. I'd sooner die.

MRS DAVENPORT (*trying to make light of it*). And I suppose you mean *that* literally too?

TONY. Yes! I'm sorry, Mum, but it's something that can only be talked about between men.

Pause.

MRS DAVENPORT. When did you become a man?

TONY. Do you remember the evening I was reading about Mrs Rattenbury and you took the paper away from me?

Pause.

MRS DAVENPORT. Yes. Very clearly. It was the evening you went to The Kensington with Randolph.

TONY. Yes. Only I didn't go to the cinema. I went – somewhere else – on my own – don't blame Randy. He warned me – he didn't want me to go –

MRS DAVENPORT *is silent and unmoving.*

I'm sorry, but that's all I can tell you.

MRS DAVENPORT. No, it isn't. A boy should be able to tell his mother *everything*.

TONY. I'm not a boy any longer, Mum. I'm grown up… A pretty horrible way to grow up, I know – but it's happened, and there it is… I went to a doctor and I know what I've got to face now.

MRS DAVENPORT. Who is this doctor?

TONY. Oh, anonymous. I'm anonymous too. Someone at St George's Hospital. There's a notice up in lavatories in Tube stations telling you where to go. I didn't have the courage until today.

MRS DAVENPORT. You should have seen Dr Macintyre –

TONY. And have him tell you?

MRS DAVENPORT. *You've* told me.

TONY. Not the lot. Not the sordid details. Not the things I've got to do in the bathroom twice a day. But not in *this* bathroom – I'm determined on that.

MRS DAVENPORT (*bravely*). Why *not* this bathroom?

TONY *smiles and shakes his head.*

… I won't say a word to you about it. I promise you… If it's not serious, if it's just something you'll get over with treatment –

TONY. Mum – twice a day for maybe six weeks, maybe longer, I'll have to lock myself in there – (*Points off.*) and you'll hear a tap running. Do you honestly think I can hope to come out of there without knowing what you're saying to yourself: 'My son has committed a filthy, disgusting act, and he's been punished for it with a filthy, disgusting disease and a filthy, disgusting treatment – '

MRS DAVENPORT (*roused*). Well, isn't that true?

TONY. No. What I did that night was silly, if you like, but the act was as natural as breathing – and a good deal more pleasant. Goodnight, Mum.

MRS DAVENPORT. Tony, don't you realise what I've got to go through tomorrow? You're not going to him now. I won't allow it.

TONY. What will you do? Get out a warrant? And have me tell the Judge about my adventure in Paddington? I'm sorry, Mum. I *am* terribly sorry. (*Goes to the door.*) Don't wait up. If he'll have me, I'll stay the night. (*Goes.*)

MRS DAVENPORT *is motionless for a moment – then suddenly she shudders – quite violently, as if she were ill.*

STELLA (*coming in*). Where's Tony?

MRS DAVENPORT (*incoherently muttering*). That… *that*… woman.

The lights fade.

Cries of 'Kill her!' 'Hang her!' Odd screams of 'Hanging's too good for her! Give her the cat too!' can also be heard.

Interspersed with barked orders from the police, and over all, the sound of JOAN, *incensed, as she roars abuse at the crowd.*

JOAN (*off*). Out of the way, you old bitch, or I'll fetch you one in the crutch – … You, you bastard, call yourself a man? Bash 'em, Officer!… What's your baton for? Hit that old cow on the conk – that's more like it! Push, push! Run, dear, run.

The lights have dimly lit a cell. A woman, seemingly a wardress, runs inside and cowers in the corner. We do not see her face.

(*Off.*) Get that door closed, Officer!

A door clangs and there is comparative silence.

(*Off.*) Bloody morons – the lot of 'em.

JOAN *comes into the cell and turns on the light simultaneously. We see she has made a gallant attempt to dress as* ALMA *might be expected to – with pretty femininity, and a decorative hat. What now spoils the effect is that the hat is over one eye, her dress is torn nearly off her and she has an incipient black eye.*

(*Cheerfully.*) Well, dear, that worked a treat, didn't it?

The huddled figure in wardress uniform reveals herself to be a very scared and bewildered ALMA.

There's no better weapon than a lady's handbag, I always say.

JOAN *drops the handbag onto a table whence it emits a sharp sound.*

Come on, now. Get out of that uniform. Your dress is here.

She throws the dress down on the table.

ALMA. They were shouting: 'Kill her!'

JOAN. You mustn't take any notice, dear. There are a lot of ill people in the world. Far more than anyone knows. Have a cup of coffee.

Out of the bag (which also contains a brick) she brings a thermos.

ALMA. Joan –

JOAN. Yes, dear?

ALMA. Why?

JOAN. God knows. I've seen it often before. Never as bad as this, I grant, but – envy, that's what I think it is – plain envy.

ALMA. How can they envy me now?

JOAN. Well, you in the Old Bailey, centre of attention… But of course, now it's hate-mob hate, which is the nastiest, illest, ugliest thing in the whole world… Mind you, I'm not the Pope. Let's get changed, dear. I don't want the lawyers to catch us like this.

ALMA (*hands to her face*). Hatred is awful!

JOAN. Forget them! It's a compliment to be hated by them. (*Spreading out the dress.*) There's the dress you wanted. You're going to look a picture in court, I know it –

The lights fade as they both dress, coming up immediately on the lawyers' robing room. Some lockers and a bench are all that is necessary. CASSWELL *is finishing robing himself as* O'CONNOR *comes in.*

O'CONNOR. Ah, Casswell, just the man I want to see. Is the enemy about?

CASSWELL. Croom-Johnson? He's just left to muster his witnesses.

O'CONNOR. And quite a crowd he's got, I gather. Was he looking cocky?

CASSWELL (*gloomily*). He's every reason to, hasn't he?

O'CONNOR. We'll see. How's your lad?

CASSWELL. Wood? I haven't seen him yet today.

O'CONNOR. Very spirited disposition, I hear.

CASSWELL. That's one word for it. I call it cheeky. Cheeky and stubborn.

O'CONNOR. A bad combination. How far are you involving us in the borrowing of the mallet?

CASSWELL. Wood's father is going to say he assumed the boy was borrowing it with your client's knowledge and consent!

O'CONNOR. Assumption is nothing. I can tear that apart. What exactly did he tell the father he was borrowing it for?

CASSWELL. To put up a sun-shelter. In the garden.

O'CONNOR. A sun-shelter? In mid-March, and on one of the coldest days of the year?

CASSWELL. Was it?

O'CONNOR. Yes.

CASSWELL. Should I have known that? Is it important?

O'CONNOR. It is to me.

CASSWELL. Why?

O'CONNOR. Trade secret, dear boy. If I thought it would help you, I'd tell you – but it won't.

CASSWELL (*suspiciously*). You look cheerful.

O'CONNOR. I always look cheerful. It's half the battle. You'd better do something about yourself. Try a little rouge or something.

CASSWELL (*looking at himself*). I didn't sleep at all last night.

O'CONNOR. That's a mistake. I had a large dinner at the Garrick, got away from the bloody actors and slept two hours in the smoking room. After that – home and bed. Now listen, Casswell, I don't want to bully, but any suggestion that we wielded that mallet and I shall not hesitate to remind the jury that while we are a poor, weak woman who couldn't drive an iron peg into soft peat in under forty whacks, you are a hulking great muscular brute of an ex-builder who can easily knock a man's head off in three.

CASSWELL (*with a resigned sigh*). Yes. And did.

O'CONNOR. That's right. And did. You're not disputing your statement of confession to the police on the day of your arrest?

CASSWELL. How can I?

O'CONNOR. I don't know. I only know I'm disputing every one of mine. After half an hour in there with the Bournemouth Constabulary those seven separate confessions will be floating down past Croom-Johnson's nose like confetti. I suppose while you were knocking the old man's block in, we were winding up the gramophone and cheering and egging you on – ?

CASSWELL. Of course. I'm sorry, O'Connor, but it's my only chance.

O'CONNOR. Of what.

CASSWELL. Of getting a manslaughter.

O'CONNOR *chuckles*.

I'd better warn you I intend to push your evil moral influence and your shameless depravity as hard as I can.

O'CONNOR. Push away, my dear fellow, push away, if it's all you've got, I'm going to push your psychopathological rages, your surliness and your fits of sudden violence. You won't mind that, I hope?

CASSWELL. The reverse. It might help me to a guilty but insane.

O'CONNOR. Under Humphreys? Not a hope. He sleeps with the McNaghten rules under his pillow. Did the murderer know what he was doing at the time that he did it? If he did, did he know that what he was doing was wrong? (*Helps himself into a pair of slippers.*) I'd say that your boy had a teeny inkling of both.

CASSWELL. Do you always wear slippers in court?

O'CONNOR. Always. Because they make us as uncomfortable as they can up here – (*Indicates his upper half.*) is no reason why we shouldn't be cosy down here. Anyway, aren't you supposed to have committed the murder under the influence of a lorryload of cocaine?

CASSWELL. Yes, damn it. He would choose the one drug that heightens the perceptions rather than dulling them.

O'CONNOR. Change your drug.

CASSWELL. I can't. Cocaine is what I'm instructed to take, and as a Poor Persons' Defence Act Lawyer, I've got to obey my instructions.

O'CONNOR (*sententiously*). My dear fellow, we all have to obey our instructions. Some of us sometimes manage to get them just a little bit – confused –

CASSWELL. Not a chance here. He won't budge an inch.

O'CONNOR. Where did you get the cocaine from?

CASSWELL. Someone somewhere in London. We can't remember who or where.

O'CONNOR. Good God. And you're stuck with his whole confession?

CASSWELL. No way round it. (*Gloomily swallows two pills.*)

O'CONNOR. Hangover?

CASSWELL. No. Nerves. Does one ever get over them?

O'CONNOR. Never. They get worse with age.

CASSWELL. I've never seen you look even remotely nervous.

O'CONNOR. Ah. That's something we do learn – never to show it. But that carafe I always have in front of me. You don't think that's plain water, do you?

CASSWELL. Gin?

O'CONNOR. Vodka. Safe as houses. Not a whiff from a foot away. Is this your first capital charge?

CASSWELL. No. But with the others I had some chance –

O'CONNOR. My dear boy, while there's life there's hope.

CASSWELL. Our hope – their lives.

Pause. O'CONNOR *turns slowly on him.*

O'CONNOR. Do you think there's a single moment I'm unconscious of that?

CASSWELL. No. Well, I'd better have one last shot at getting him to change his drug into something else.

O'CONNOR. Yes. Good luck. (*Suddenly savage.*) But look, Casswell!

CASSWELL *turns.*

If there's the faintest suggestion that he got any drugs from her, I'll be on you like a tiger. That poor bitch has got enough to carry into the court without dope-peddling. (*Puts his hand on* CASSWELL*'s arm.*) Get him to come off drugs altogether. Use our shameless depravity and pernicious influence. It's much safer. And I can't hit back. That's my honest advice, old man.

CASSWELL (*with a sigh*). Well, it would be a very foolish advocate who neglected advice from such a source. Thank you.

O'CONNOR. You're very welcome.

CASSWELL *is on his way out when a thought strikes him.*

CASSWELL. Unless such a source happened to be fighting the same trial with him.

O'CONNOR. As an ally, dear fellow –

CASSWELL. An ally who wouldn't hesitate to slash my throat if he thought it could help his client.

O'CONNOR. Slash your throat, my dear Casswell, I've just given you an open invitation to attack me in my weakest spot, to wit, my deplorable moral character. Now, how could that possibly be slashing your throat?

MONTAGU – *who is already gowned – comes in.*

Ah, Montagu. Good. (*With an innocent smile.*) Have you got our friend in all right?

The lights fade on O'CONNOR *and* MONTAGU *and stay on* CASSWELL *as he walks unhappily towards a small cell,*

where the lights come on to show WOOD *sitting patiently.*
O'CONNOR *and* MONTAGU *disappear from view.*

CASSWELL (*calls*). Warder!

WOOD (*chirpily*). Morning, Mr Casswell. Did you hear that
crowd cheering me when I arrived? Some of them shouted
'Good luck, lad' – and 'We won't let you swing' – things
like that…

CASSWELL. Mr Wood, we have only a few minutes before
you go on trial for your life. Are you still determined to
instruct me that you murdered Rattenbury when under the
influence of cocaine?

Pause.

WOOD. Perce Wood, the odd-job boy, has come a long way,
hasn't he, instructing someone dressed up like you… Well, I
instruct you, Mr Casswell, I done the old man in when I was
crazed from cocaine and not responsible for my actions. And
that's what I'm going to tell them.

CASSWELL. You won't have the opportunity. I am not putting
you in the witness box.

WOOD. How can you stop me?

CASSWELL. By not calling you.

WOOD. Why not? You've got to!

CASSWELL. I am not putting you into the witness box because
I would not like to hear you explaining to Mr Croom-
Johnson, one of the most devastating cross-examiners at the
Bar, exactly how you became 'a dope fiend'.

WOOD. But that's my defence!

CASSWELL. What does cocaine look like? Mr Wood? I mean,
what colour is it?

WOOD. Colour? (*After a pause.*) Brown.

CASSWELL. Brown.

WOOD. With black specks.

CASSWELL. With black specks... And if you went into the witness box you would tell Mr Croom-Johnson that?

WOOD. Of course.

CASSWELL. And if he asked you why, in popular parlance, it was called 'snow', how would you answer him?

WOOD. I don't know – I didn't know it was.

CASSWELL. It is called snow because it is white, Mr Wood – the purest possible *white*.

Pause.

WOOD. Jesus.

CASSWELL. Exactly.

WOOD. But without cocaine, where's my defence?

CASSWELL. I've told you – many times.

Pause.

WOOD (*violently*). No!

CASSWELL. You are of age to be hanged, Mr Wood.

WOOD. I know.

CASSWELL. You are disposed then to die?

WOOD. No, I'm not. I want to live – Christ, don't I want to live. But I'm not going to say *she* made me do it. They can tear me apart before they'll get me to say that.

CASSWELL. I don't think you quite understand –

WOOD (*violently*). It's you who don't bloody understand. Alma Rattenbury, sex-mad drunken bloody cow that she is, lying deceitful bitch to come to that – she's the only woman I've ever had, and the only one I've ever loved, and I'm not going to shop her now... No, it's you who don't bloody understand, Mr Casswell, nor the others either.

Pause.

CASSWELL. Very likely. I'll see you in court.

CASSWELL *picks up his brief. The lights fade, coming up immediately on the other cell.* ALMA *is now dressed.*

JOAN. Not long now, dear. I said you'd look a treat.

O'CONNOR *and* MONTAGU *come in, gowned, and carrying their wigs.*

O'CONNOR. Wardress – bring Mrs Rattenbury, please.

JOAN. Sir.

MONTAGU (*to* ALMA). I hope they didn't upset you too much outside.

ALMA. Well, it came as rather a shock –

O'CONNOR. Mrs Rattenbury, it is my duty to tell you that there will be deep prejudice against you up there.

ALMA. Oh, I know.

O'CONNOR. Very deep indeed, I'm afraid. You must be prepared to answer some very venomous questions.

ALMA (*simply*). Oh, but I'm not going to answer any questions. I'm not going into the witness box. I told you that, Mr Montagu.

Pause. O'CONNOR *makes a sign to* MONTAGU *who slips out of the room.*

O'CONNOR. I beg you most earnestly to reconsider, madam.

ALMA. I'm sorry. I can't. I will not go into the witness box. *Not* under oath. *Not* giving George away…

O'CONNOR. Because you want him to see you as a tragic heroine? You love him as much as that?

ALMA. Me a heroine to George?… That's funny. To him I'm just a drunken sexy lying bitch. He's told me so a million times.

O'CONNOR. Then why in heaven's name sacrifice yourself for him?

ALMA. Because it's right. I'm *responsible*, and neither you nor anyone…

MONTAGU *brings* CHRISTOPHER *in.*

CHRISTOPHER. Hello, Mummy.

ALMA *stands still for a moment, then turns furiously on* O'CONNOR.

ALMA. What kind of a man are you?

O'CONNOR. A humane man, Mrs Rattenbury. I thought you might like a couple of minutes with your boy before you go into court…

With a curt beckoning nod he ushers MONTAGU *out, following him.*

CHRISTOPHER. What's Mr O'Connor done, Mummy? What's made you angry with him?

ALMA. Never mind. (*Embraces him.*) How are you, Chris?

CHRISTOPHER. Oh, all right.

ALMA. They brought you up from school?

CHRISTOPHER. I wanted to come. (*Looking at her.*) You're in an ordinary dress…

ALMA. Yes. Do you like it?

CHRISTOPHER. Yes. It's nice. I thought –

ALMA. That I'd be in stripes and arrows? Not yet.

CHRISTOPHER. What's it like in prison?

ALMA. Oh, it's not really prison. And the wardresses – the people I'm with – they're very nice. (*Suddenly clutching him.*) They didn't bring you through those crowds?

CHRISTOPHER. Oh yes – but nobody knew who *I* was. They were nasty people, though.

ALMA. Did you hear them shouting?

CHRISTOPHER (*quickly*). Oh, I didn't listen, Mummy.

She clutches him fiercely again, then lets him go.

ALMA. And how's little John?

CHRISTOPHER. Oh, all right. He gets a bit tearful, sometimes.

ALMA. They haven't told him –

CHRISTOPHER. Oh no.

ALMA. He misses me?

CHRISTOPHER. *Misses* you?

Pause.

ALMA (*trying to steady her voice*). Well, Chris, what have you been told to say to me?

CHRISTOPHER (*bewildered*). Told to say to you?

ALMA. By Mr O'Connor?

CHRISTOPHER. Nothing.

ALMA. Really? Nothing?

CHRISTOPHER. Well, the obvious thing, of course.

ALMA. What's that?

CHRISTOPHER. About your not giving George away in court. It was a bit of a shock, because he says the jury may find you guilty; but he put it so nicely, though…

ALMA (*faintly*). How did he put it?

CHRISTOPHER. Well, he said that as a schoolboy I'd understand about not sneaking on a friend… Well, of course I understand, except in this kind of thing… I mean, in a case of murder – real murder – what they might do – except, of course, they'd never do that to you… Oh, Mummy!…

He runs to her. She clasps him firmly and allows him to cry on her breast.

Oh, damn! I promised I wouldn't.

ALMA (*at length*). What else did Mr O'Connor put 'so nicely'?

CHRISTOPHER. He said that as I was nearly grown up I should understand that when a woman has a choice between her lover and her children, she's almost bound to put her lover first.

ALMA, *apparently unmoved and unmoving, looks down at his head.*

O'CONNOR *and* MONTAGU *come back.* ALMA *has not moved.*

O'CONNOR. The Judge has sent us his signal. (*Puts his arm on* CHRISTOPHER*'s shoulder.*) You should be getting to your seat, young man. A Mr Watson, outside, will be sitting with you –

ALMA (*appalled*). Christopher's not going to be in court?

O'CONNOR. Of course.

ALMA. Will he be there every day?

O'CONNOR. That depends. Say au revoir to your mother, old chap.

CHRISTOPHER. Goodbye, Mummy. Good luck.

O'CONNOR. Montagu, you take him to Watson – Wardress!

ALMA *lets* CHRISTOPHER *kiss her, patting him absently on the head as he goes out with* MONTAGU.

ALMA (*at length*). Don't think you've won, Mr O'Connor.

O'CONNOR. Oh, I never think that about any case, until the end.

End of Act One.

ACT TWO

As at the beginning of Act One, the lights come up on ALMA *and* MRS DAVENPORT.

A light then comes up on the JUDGE.

JUDGE. Mrs – er – Davenport, I understand from the Jury Bailiff that you wish to be excused from jury service on the grounds of conscience?

MRS DAVENPORT. Yes. From this particular jury, on this particular case. I will serve on any other.

JUDGE. You have a conscientious objection to capital punishment?

MRS DAVENPORT. No, my lord.

JUDGE. Where then does your conscience enter the matter?

MRS DAVENPORT. My lord, I have a deep prejudice against that woman. (*Acknowledges the dock.*)

JUDGE. The female prisoner?

MRS DAVENPORT. Yes.

JUDGE. Would the female prisoner please rise?

ALMA *rises. She stares at* MRS DAVENPORT *without surprise – even with faint understanding.*

Do you know this woman personally?

MRS DAVENPORT. No, but it's as if I did.

JUDGE. I don't follow, I'm afraid.

MRS DAVENPORT. I've read about her in the newspapers.

Pause.

JUDGE. Is that all?

998 7 6 5 4 3 2 1

The lights come up dimly on the lawyers.

MRS DAVENPORT. My lord, you are here to see that this woman gets a fair trial. Isn't that so?

JUDGE. It is, madam. It is also my duty, as it will be yours, to put out of my head all of the deplorably wide publicity this case has attracted, and to allow the facts of the case –

MRS DAVENPORT. I am sorry, my lord. I know these arguments. You see, I know about the law. My father was a judge in India –

JUDGE. Mrs – er – but I don't –

MRS DAVENPORT (*passionately*). I warn you now, and I warn these gentlemen who are defending her, that no matter what oath I am forced to take, I will not be able to try this woman's case without deep prejudice. My mind is set against her.

Pause. Her sincerity has evidently impressed the JUDGE. *He frowns thoughtfully and then addresses the lawyers' bench. As he does so, the lights fade except on* ALMA *and* MRS DAVENPORT.

The discussion between the JUDGE *and the lawyers is only dimly heard.*

JUDGE. Mr O'Connor, you have heard my view. It remains unaltered. However, you might have cause for a challenge '*propter affectum*'. If you have I am very willing to hear it.

O'CONNOR. If your lordship permits?

The JUDGE *nods.* O'CONNOR *talks to* MONTAGU *in a low voice, their backs to the* JUDGE.

MONTAGU. She's an asset.

O'CONNOR. On the question of bias?

MONTAGU. Exactly. You can refer to her in your final address.

He rises again.

O'CONNOR. My lord, we will not challenge.

CASSWELL. No challenge, my lord. The prejudice does not appear to be directed against my client.

JUDGE. Obviously, Mr Croom-Johnson, you won't wish to challenge. But do you think I am right?

CROOM-JOHNSON, *prosecuting counsel, gets up*.

CROOM-JOHNSON. I feel your lordship's view of the matter is both wise and just.

The light comes up on the JUDGE.

JUDGE. Mrs Davenport, we all find that there are no grounds for your self-disqualification. Will you then take the oath?

CLERK OF THE COURT. Take the book in your right hand and repeat the words on the cards.

The lights fade on the JUDGE *and the lawyers.*

Now only the two women can be seen facing each other across the courtroom.

MRS DAVENPORT (*solemnly, after a pause, the Bible in her right hand, a card in the other*). I do solemnly swear by Almighty God that I will well and truly try the issues between our Sovereign Lord the King and the prisoners at the bar and will give a true verdict according to the evidence.

The lights fade quickly to blackout.

In the sitting room, STELLA *is dimly seen reading a newspaper. The lights come up on Court Number One at the Old Bailey. The court is not in session. The lawyers are chatting.*

CASSWELL (*to* CROOM-JOHNSON). Congratulations on your opening.

CROOM-JOHNSON. Oh, thank you, Casswell, thank you.

CASSWELL. Admirably fair, I thought.

CROOM-JOHNSON. I'm glad.

O'CONNOR (*muttering some distance away, to* MONTAGU). 'Fair'! If that bloody Croom-Johnson uses the phrase

'woman and *boy*' once more, I'm going to have him
disbarred and demand a retrial –

MONTAGU. Why don't you tell him?

O'CONNOR. And let him know he's scored? We'll have
'woman and *child*' then…

CROOM-JOHNSON *moves near.*

(*Calling.*) Good opening, Croom-Johnson.

CROOM-JOHNSON. Thank you. It was fair, I think.

O'CONNOR. Every bit as fair as we've come to expect of you.

CROOM-JOHNSON. How kind. Extraordinary incident that
was – that woman juror saying she was prejudiced against
your client. Very distressing to hear that kind of thing, you
know. I wonder you didn't challenge.

O'CONNOR. Yes. I suppose I should have done –

CROOM-JOHNSON (*suspiciously*). You won't, of course, be
able to make any reference to her in your final address –

O'CONNOR. Oh no. That would be most deeply improper.

CROOM-JOHNSON. Well, I honestly think my opening will
have helped remove some of her prejudices –

O'CONNOR. Yes.

CROOM-JOHNSON. I emphasised that this was in no way a
court of morals – and that they were to direct their attention
only to the facts of the case.

O'CONNOR (*unable to contain himself*). – brought against
'this woman and this boy' –

CROOM-JOHNSON. Ah. I did notice your uneasiness at the
appellation 'boy'. But what else in all honesty could I call
him, O'Connor? The jury have only to look at the dock –

O'CONNOR. – and see a hulking young man, old enough to be
hanged, and a woman young-looking enough to pass herself
off successfully as his sister.

CROOM-JOHNSON. But the gap in ages is so much a part of the case. One must steel oneself, must one not, to face facts, however disagreeable. (*Gathers up his papers.*)

O'CONNOR. Bloody man! – Do you know I drew him in the Bar golf tournament, and he wouldn't give me a fourteen-inch putt?... I missed it too. I've got to beat that bugger – (*Smiles at* CROOM-JOHNSON *as he passes again.*) if it's the last thing I do.

As the lawyers leave the court, the lights fade, coming up as MRS DAVENPORT *enters wearily.* STELLA, *lying on a sofa, is reading an evening newspaper.*

MRS DAVENPORT. Has Tony come home?

STELLA. Tony? No.

MRS DAVENPORT. Oh, God, I won't let John take him away from me, I won't, I won't. (*Sits on sofa.*)

STELLA. Darling, you've had a tiring day. Do you want a cup of tea?

MRS DAVENPORT. No, but I'd love a drink. A whisky.

STELLA. That's bold of you. (*Gets up to pour the whisky.*) So it didn't work this morning?

MRS DAVENPORT. No. And what's worse, the jury has elected me Forewoman because I'd let out that father was a judge.

STELLA. My dear, how too splendid. What d'you have in court tomorrow?

MRS DAVENPORT. The rest of the prosecution witnesses, I think. Oh, Stella, it's all so foul.

She goes out to the bedroom. STELLA *picks up her newspaper and crosses to the phone.*

STELLA (*calling*). Darling, do you know what odds the bookmakers are laying on Mrs Rattenbury being convicted?

MRS DAVENPORT (*off*). 'Odds'? How can they be so unfeeling?

STELLA. No principles, bookmakers. In the city they're even taking bets on whether she'll hang. Good odds too. But for her being convicted – it's here somewhere. (*Looks in the paper*.) Yes, they're giving three to one.

MRS DAVENPORT (*off*). Only three to one? That woman – it's absurd.

STELLA. Well – if ever I heard a tip straight from the horse's mouth – (*Into phone*.) Hello – still at the office? There's a good Henry!… Look, darling, apparently you can get three to one on Mrs Rattenbury being convicted – well – (*Lowering her voice*.) Edie's just back from court, and she says that in her view those odds are madly generous… Yes, and they've made her Forewoman too, so of course she'll have a big say… Yes, a real hot snip. Well, put on six hundred for me, would you?…

TONY *comes in*.

Thank you, darling… I will. Henry sends his love. (*Hangs up*.) Tony!

TONY. Hullo, Aunt Stella.

MRS DAVENPORT *comes back in, wearing a dressing gown*.

MRS DAVENPORT. Tony!

TONY.… Hullo, Mum.

MRS DAVENPORT. Tony, thank God. You've come back.

TONY. No, I haven't. Dad's here.

MRS DAVENPORT. I won't see him!

JOHN DAVENPORT *enters*.

I'm not allowed to see you. The Judge said –

DAVENPORT. I remember very well what the Judge said. 'No communication of any kind.' Hullo, Stella.

STELLA. Hullo, John.

DAVENPORT. So this letter I've brought is just as wrong as my presence. (*Holds out a letter.*)

MRS DAVENPORT. I won't read it.

DAVENPORT. I thought not, which is why I'm delivering it myself.

STELLA. I'll go.

MRS DAVENPORT. No, don't. Please.

DAVENPORT. I don't mind Stella hearing what I've got to say. Tony, go down and wait in the car, would you?

MRS DAVENPORT. Are you taking him away?

DAVENPORT. To the cottage.

MRS DAVENPORT. And I forbid him to go.

DAVENPORT. Go ahead, Tony.

MRS DAVENPORT. No –

TONY. Sorry, Mum. Really. I'll call you tomorrow. (*Goes*.)

MRS DAVENPORT. I've only to ring the police –

DAVENPORT. Yes. Then I'd have to give my exact reasons to the Judge for taking my son away from here. Of course he'd find the reasons quite insufficient, and I'd be fined or committed, and Tony would be returned to you. There'd probably be a little something in the papers, which probably would be read by Tony's headmaster –

MRS DAVENPORT. This is pure blackmail.

DAVENPORT. Yes it is, I suppose. It's also a truthful forecast of what would happen, must happen, if you invoke the law.

MRS DAVENPORT. Exactly what lies have you told his headmaster?

DAVENPORT. I told him the truth. Not all of it, but I said the boy had had a severe psychological shock, that he'd attempted suicide –

MRS DAVENPORT. That's a lie!

DAVENPORT. It's not. The night before last he swallowed some sleeping pills.

MRS DAVENPORT. No –

DAVENPORT. If you don't believe me, go into the bathroom and look for your sleeping pills. Luckily there were only seven or eight left, and they made him sick at once.

MRS DAVENPORT. But I'd have heard if –

DAVENPORT. Tony's a polite boy. He can even vomit quietly enough not to wake his mother. And then apparently lie on the bathroom floor, sobbing – but into a towel, quietly.

MRS DAVENPORT. But is this – thing he has as dreadful as that?

DAVENPORT. Medically it's nothing, provided it's treated promptly… It's the psychological shock he won't get over so easily, and he'd never get over it here… unless…

Pause.

Are you going to read my letter?

MRS DAVENPORT. Never.

DAVENPORT. Then I'll read it to you. (*Takes the letter and opens it.*) 'My dearest Edie – for the sake of Tony, and also for our own sakes, I want you to rescind the decree nisi. It's very easily done, by application to a judge in chambers.

I must tell you with complete truth that there is no other woman in my life. No single other woman, that is. The one you know about left me some months ago, with no regrets on either side. She wasn't important to me. No woman has ever been important to me except yourself. I admit that I've had occasional affairs, but they were necessary to me – you know why – always brief, and usually with a mercenary tinge.

Without you, Edie, and without Tony, I have been a very lonely man. So, I believe, are you lonely without me. Please let me come back into your life. If you do I promise to behave as well as I can. That doesn't, I'm afraid, mean as well as you'd want me to. It can never mean that, Edie my darling, as you know. But if you can only bring yourself to overlook an occasional late night at the office, or the odd dinner at the Club with the Permanent Secretary, I swear a solemn oath to

you that you will never otherwise be humiliated. I renounce
my conjugal rights entirely, but I earnestly entreat you to let
me once again be your loving husband.

John.'

*He puts it back in the envelope and hands it to her. She won't
take it. He puts it on the coffee table.*

MRS DAVENPORT. Your terms.

DAVENPORT. Yours as well.

MRS DAVENPORT. The answer is no.

STELLA. Think about it, Edie. For God's sake, think about it.

MRS DAVENPORT. Stella, how can you? He wants me to –
condone adultery? It's unthinkable and you know it, I will
not break the standards by which I've lived all my life.

DAVENPORT. Those standards could be wrong, you know.
They're certainly becoming a little dated... You won't
reconsider?

No reply.

Well, I'll say goodbye. (*At the door.*) Tell me – this Mrs
Rattenbury, is she for it?

MRS DAVENPORT. We're not allowed to talk about it.

DAVENPORT (*smiling*). I don't give much for her chances with
you judging her. I don't know anything about Mrs
Rattenbury, except what I've read in the papers, but that's
enough to tell me that her vices, which I am sure are
deplorable, do add up to some kind of affirmation. Your
virtues, Edie, which I know are admirable, add up to
precisely nothing. Goodbye!

He goes. MRS DAVENPORT *picks up the letter, then tears it
up decisively. The lights fade as she goes to her room.*
STELLA *picks up the pieces of the letter, then sits.*

The Old Bailey. The trial is in its second day, and POLICE
SERGEANT BAGWELL *is being examined by* CROOM-
JOHNSON *for the prosecution. The dock is unseen.*

CROOM-JOHNSON. At what time did you receive this call from the hospital? You may use your notebook, if there is no objection.

CASSWELL *and the* JUDGE *both nod acceptance.*

O'CONNOR *is too busy muttering to* MONTAGU *to notice.*

SERGEANT. The call came through at 2.13 a.m., sir, saying that all attempts to revive the deceased had failed.

CROOM-JOHNSON. What did you do then?

SERGEANT. Acting on this information, I duly presented myself at the Villa Madeira, at 2.47 a.m. There was a lot of commotion proceeding from inside –

CROOM-JOHNSON. What kind of commotion?

The lights fade to a spot on the SERGEANT.

SERGEANT. There was a gramophone playing at full blast, sir – and some female laughter of a shrill nature. There being no answer to the bell, I tried the door and found it open. I then entered the sitting room, and found the female prisoner attired in a nightdress, and two police officers to whom she was making flourishing gestures with her bed jacket – in imitation of bullfighting or some such. I immediately summoned the two officers outside, asked what their business had been, and sent them away. I then proceeded back into the house.

The lights have come up on the sitting room of the Villa Madeira where ALMA, *dressed as described by the* SERGEANT, *is continuing her cavortings to a now empty room. The gramophone is playing loudly. Suddenly she notices.*

ALMA. Oh, damn and blast! (*Plaintively.*) Where have you gone? Come back. We're having fun.

She takes a large swig from an evidently almost empty bottle. The record runs out and she goes to change it. She is very drunk. The SERGEANT *comes in, knocking politely at the open door.* ALMA, *at the gramophone, has her back to him.*

SERGEANT. Beg pardon for the intrusion, but would you be –

ALMA (*with a shriek of joy*). Oh, another lovely policeman! Come in. Come in. We're having a gorgeous time –

The deafening music has started up again.

SERGEANT (*shouting*). Would you be Mrs Francis Rattenbury?

ALMA. Alma to you, dear. Come and dance –

She puts her arms round his neck. He detaches himself.

SERGEANT. May we have the music down, please?

ALMA. Why? How can we dance with no music?

She tries again to get him to dance. Again he eludes.

SERGEANT. Excuse me, madam. With your permission?

He goes to the gramophone and turns it off.

ALMA. Oh, why did you do that? Now it's quiet. I don't like it quiet –

She goes to the gramophone again. He gently restrains her.

SERGEANT. I'm sorry, madam, but you could be disturbing the neighbours.

ALMA (*laughing*). Oh, that's terrible. Disturbing the neighbours is terrible.

SERGEANT. I must ask you again if you are Mrs Francis Rattenbury?

ALMA. That's right.

SERGEANT. The widow of Francis Rattenbury.

ALMA. Widow?

SERGEANT. You have not been informed of your husband's death?

ALMA. Don't talk about awful things. Let's have some music –

SERGEANT (*restraining her*). I must ask you, madam, what you know about your husband's death.

ALMA. Everything. I know everything. (*Shudders and covers her face, then emerges brightly smiling.*) I did it, you see. All by myself. All alone. (*Singing and dancing.*) All alone, all alone.

She goes to the bottle. The SERGEANT *takes it from her.*

SERGEANT. Who else is in this house?

ALMA. Only Irene.

SERGEANT. Irene?

ALMA. She's my maid. My friend. I sent her up to bed. She knows nothing about it. I want my whisky –

ALMA *takes the bottle from him. She seems to finish it.*

SERGEANT. And this Irene is the only other person in the house?

ALMA, *in the act of looking for another bottle, stops and turns slowly.*

ALMA. There's George too –

SERGEANT. George?

ALMA. My chauffeur. He's only a boy. He's nothing – just an odd-job boy –

SERGEANT. Where is he?

ALMA. How would I know? I'm not his mother… I expect he's upstairs, asleep. He's very young, you see –

SERGEANT. Madam, I must now caution you. You are not obliged to say anything unless you wish to do so, but whatever you do say will be taken down and may be given in evidence. Do you follow me?

ALMA. Anywhere. Are you married? You've lots of girls, I expect – Would you like ten pounds? No, it's a crime to give a policeman money.

SERGEANT. Madam, please.

ALMA. He wanted to die, you see. He said he'd lived too long. He gave me a mallet and dared me to kill him, so I did.

SERGEANT. Where is the mallet?

ALMA (*yawning*). What?

SERGEANT. The mallet? Where is the mallet?

ALMA. Oh, I'll remember in the morning. (*Gets up.*) No, mustn't sleep. I might dream. Let's have that music again –

SERGEANT (*closing his notebook*). Madam, I propose to telephone the police station, using the call box outside –

ALMA. There's one in there. Better still, there's one in the bedroom.

SERGEANT. I shall use the call box, thank you, madam.

ALMA. Please yourself, but you don't know what you're missing –

The SERGEANT *goes out. As he disappears,* ALMA *is going towards the gramophone. After he has left she covers her face, emitting a sob, as reality seems to hit her. Then, swaying, she places the record back on the turntable and the music starts up again, deafeningly loud.*

The lights fade as she moves in time to the music, and come up on the courtroom. The SERGEANT *is continuing his evidence. The music overlaps until it too fades out.*

CROOM-JOHNSON. A general question, Sergeant, about Mrs Rattenbury's behaviour. Remembering that only a few hours before, her husband had been brutally killed, how did you react in your mind to her attitude that night?

SERGEANT. I was – disgusted, sir.

CROOM-JOHNSON. In one word, how would you describe her behaviour?

SERGEANT (*after thought*). Callous. Downright brutal.

CROOM-JOHNSON. Thank you, Sergeant.

He sits down.

MONTAGU. Look at the press boys scampering out. Imagine the headlines.

O'CONNOR. They should have waited. (*Rises*.) Sergeant, how long have you been in the police force?

SERGEANT. Twenty years, sir.

O'CONNOR. In that time you would, of course, have attended at many gruesome occasions – car accidents and the like?

SERGEANT. Yes, sir. Many.

O'CONNOR. You must then be familiar with the medical phenomenon known as shock?

SERGEANT. I've seen cases of shock, sir.

O'CONNOR. Severe shock?

SERGEANT. Some severe.

O'CONNOR. How do such persons usually behave?

SERGEANT. Well, I'd say, sometimes they're not quite all there.

O'CONNOR. 'Not quite all there'? Not aware of their surroundings, or excited and over-talkative?

SERGEANT. Both, sir.

O'CONNOR. Inclined to fits either of hysterical weeping or, quite as likely, hysterical laughter – and, generally speaking, inclined to behave entirely out of character?

SERGEANT. Yes, sir.

O'CONNOR. Why then were you so disgusted at Mrs Rattenbury's behaviour that night?

SERGEANT. I didn't think it was shock, sir. I mean, I saw no occasion –

O'CONNOR. You 'saw no occasion'? Can you imagine a greater occasion for shock than the brutal murder of a dearly loved husband in her own home? Can you?

SERGEANT. She didn't seem disturbed, sir. Like I said – she was laughing, and dancing and playing about.

O'CONNOR (*forcefully*). Good God, man – have you never heard of hysteria?

JUDGE. Mr O'Connor.

O'CONNOR. I'm sorry, my lord. Have you never heard of hysteria, Sergeant?

SERGEANT. Of course, sir.

O'CONNOR. What form does it take?

SERGEANT. Laughing, sir. But this wasn't hysterical laughing –

O'CONNOR. And who are you to judge?

SERGEANT. I've seen hysteria, sir –

O'CONNOR. You've also seen shock, and you failed to recognise that, didn't you? What is the treatment for shock? (*As* SERGEANT *hesitates*.) Come on. You've read your manual. What does it say?

SERGEANT. One should keep the victim warm, using blankets when obtainable –

O'CONNOR. This victim was half-dressed, on a night in March. Was there a fire in the grate?

SERGEANT. No, sir.

O'CONNOR. Were the windows open?

SERGEANT. Yes, sir.

O'CONNOR. Do you remember what the temperature was that night in Bournemouth?

SERGEANT. No, sir. Not exactly.

O'CONNOR. Would it surprise you to learn that at two o'clock on the morning of March twenty-fifth, the temperature on the Town Hall roof was recorded as three degrees below freezing?

SERGEANT. I remember it was a bit chilly, sir. I didn't know it was as cold as that.

O'CONNOR. It *was* as cold as that. And the windows in the sitting room were open?

SERGEANT. Yes, sir.

O'CONNOR. Back to the manual. If the victim is *not* kept warm, what does it say can happen to the victim? What is there a danger of?

SERGEANT. Collapse, sir.

O'CONNOR. What happened to Mrs Rattenbury later that night?

SERGEANT. She did collapse, sir, and had to be put to bed – but that was the whisky.

O'CONNOR. Was it, indeed? And how much whisky did Mrs Rattenbury have to drink that night?

SERGEANT. I don't know, exactly, sir – she was drinking from the bottle, sir – and emptied it.

O'CONNOR. In front of you, Sergeant?

SERGEANT. Yes, sir.

O'CONNOR. And you allowed that?

SERGEANT. I had no option, sir.

O'CONNOR. 'No option'? What does your handbook tell you to prevent the victim taking at all costs?

Pause.

SERGEANT. Alcohol, sir.

O'CONNOR. And why, Sergeant? Do you remember why?

Pause.

SERGEANT (*quoting from memory*). Because the effect of alcohol on a shocked system will greatly increase the symptoms, and will in all respects prove strongly deleterious.

O'CONNOR. And – doesn't it add – sometimes fatal?

SERGEANT. Yes, sir.

O'CONNOR. It may be that you are lucky that in this case it was not. Otherwise you could be facing a very grave charge, Sergeant – gross negligence while on duty. That's all.

He sits down. CROOM-JOHNSON *rises.*

CROOM-JOHNSON. Sergeant, has a person in a state of shock ever made sexual advances to you?

SERGEANT. Certainly not, sir.

CROOM-JOHNSON. Or attempted to bribe you?

SERGEANT. No, sir.

CROOM-JOHNSON. Thank you, Sergeant.

The SERGEANT *descends from the box.*

That concludes the case for the Crown, my lord. (*Sits down.*)

JUDGE. Mr O'Connor. Are you ready?

O'CONNOR. Yes, my lord.

O'CONNOR *mutters to* MONTAGU, *then shrugs. He rises.*

May it please your lordship, members of the jury, it is my intention to call one witness and one witness only – namely Mrs Rattenbury. I shall therefore claim the right of the last word –

CROOM-JOHNSON (*rising swiftly*). My lord, this sudden manoeuvre of my learned friend puts me at a grave disadvantage.

O'CONNOR. My lord, I have to confess that I do not know – even at this very second, as I stand here to begin Mrs Rattenbury's defence, whether she will in fact obey my summons to the box or not. If she does not, then it is I who will stand at a grave disadvantage –

CROOM-JOHNSON. My lord, I think an adjournment at this juncture would be the right –

O'CONNOR (*angrily*). It would be most damnably wrong! – Forgive me, my lord, but I am not exaggerating when I say that in this moment – this exact moment – lies the hinge of this entire trial. Any delay, even of half an hour, might be fatal to the cause of justice. In my view it is vital that my client goes into the witness box to give evidence on her own behalf, as she has the right and, I have told her, the duty to do. I believe and pray that if called upon now, she will go. With your lordship's permission. I therefore call Alma Rattenbury.

There is a pause. ALMA *enters, and walking as if in a daze, goes to the witness box. In the box a board is handed to her and a Bible.*

CLERK OF THE COURT. Take the book in your right hand and repeat the following words, after me. I swear by Almighty God –

ALMA. I swear by Almighty God –

CLERK OF THE COURT. – that the evidence I shall give to the court –

ALMA. – that the evidence I shall give to the court –

CLERK OF THE COURT. – shall be the truth, the whole truth, and nothing but the truth.

ALMA. – shall be the truth, the whole truth, and nothing but the truth.

O'CONNOR. You are Alma Victoria Rattenbury.

ALMA. I am.

O'CONNOR. Mrs Rattenbury, how long were you married to your husband?

ALMA. Eight years.

O'CONNOR. By him did you have a child?

ALMA. Yes. Little John.

JUDGE. Mrs Rattenbury, I can't hear you. Speak up, please. And please make sure the jury can hear what you say.

ALMA. I'm sorry. I'm sorry.

O'CONNOR. Mrs Rattenbury – little John, how old is he?

ALMA. Six – (*Louder.*) Six.

O'CONNOR. And you have been married twice before, I think?

ALMA. Yes.

O'CONNOR. By the second husband you had a child, did you not?

ALMA. Yes. Christopher.

O'CONNOR. You are fond of him, I think.

ALMA. Yes.

O'CONNOR. Very fond?

ALMA. ... Very fond.

O'CONNOR. Now, Mrs Rattenbury, I want you to tell me about your relationship with your husband. Since the birth of –

ALMA. Er – (*Looks towards the public gallery.*)

O'CONNOR. Mrs Rattenbury?

ALMA. No, I –

JUDGE. Is something wrong, Mr O'Connor?

O'CONNOR. I'm sorry, my lord. An oversight on my part. If your lordship permits –

He turns to MONTAGU.

(*Murmuring.*) Get the boy out of court, will you...

MONTAGU *nods and goes.*

I do apologise, my lord. Now, Mrs Rattenbury, would you say your married life was happy?... Mrs Rattenbury!

ALMA. I'm sorry?

ALMA looks at the court, then...

O'CONNOR. Would you say your married life was happy?

ALMA. Well, it was a bit – you know –

She makes a gesture indicating 'up and down'.

O'CONNOR. You had some quarrels?

ALMA. Not many. Only little ones, and always about money. He was a bit – well – stingy. I often had to tell him little fibs to get the bills paid.

O'CONNOR. Yes. Well, we'll come back to that.

MONTAGU *returns and nods to* O'CONNOR. ALMA *again looks into the court, but clearly* CHRISTOPHER *has gone.*

Mrs Rattenbury, I want you to tell us now about your relationship with your late husband. Be quite frank, please. Since the birth of little John six years ago, did you and Mr Rattenbury live together as husband and wife?

ALMA. No.

JUDGE. Mrs Rattenbury, I must ask you to speak much louder, please. And please address your replies so the jury may hear them.

ALMA. I'm sorry.

O'CONNOR. Since that time you did not live together as husband and wife at all?

ALMA. No.

JUDGE. Mrs Rattenbury, you do understand what was meant by the question?

ALMA. Yes.

O'CONNOR. Did your husband have a separate room?

ALMA. Yes.

O'CONNOR. Was that at his suggestion or yours?

ALMA. Oh, his.

O'CONNOR. You would have been ready to continue marital relations with him?

ALMA, Oh yes, of course.

O'CONNOR. But he didn't want it?

ALMA. Well, I think it was rather a question of the flesh being willing but the spirit being weak –

O'CONNOR. Er – the other way round I think?

ALMA. I expect so.

O'CONNOR. Now, between the months of November 1934 and March 1935, were you having regular sexual intercourse with Wood?

ALMA. Yes.

Again she has a quick look into the court.

O'CONNOR. And what attitude did your husband take to all this?

ALMA. None whatsoever.

JUDGE. You mean he didn't know of it?

ALMA. Oh, I think he must have known of it, my lord.

JUDGE. Then he must have taken some attitude – even if it was one of tactful silence?

ALMA. I just don't think he gave it a thought.

The JUDGE *makes a heavy note.*

O'CONNOR. Now, Mrs Rattenbury, I am going to take you through the events of the week that led up to your husband's murder and I want you to answer my questions with complete truth. You will, will you not?

ALMA *doesn't reply.*

JUDGE. Mrs Rattenbury, you are under oath. You must reply fully and truthfully to Counsel's questions.

Again ALMA *doesn't reply.*

O'CONNOR. On Monday March eighteenth – that is six days before the murder – did you ask your husband for some money?... Mrs Rattenbury?

JUDGE. One moment, please. Mrs Rattenbury, you do understand, do you not, that having taken the oath to tell the truth, the whole truth, and nothing but the truth, you are in law in duty bound to do so. Do you understand that?

ALMA. Yes, my lord.

JUDGE. Then be so good as to answer Counsel's question.

O'CONNOR. For how much money did you ask?

Pause.

ALMA. Two hundred and fifty pounds.

O'CONNOR. What 'little fib' – to quote your words – did you
have to tell him?

ALMA. That I was going up to London to have an operation.

O'CONNOR. And on the following day you went up to
London?

ALMA. Yes.

O'CONNOR. And you stayed with Wood at an hotel in
Kensington?

ALMA. Yes. The Royal Palace.

O'CONNOR. During that time did you give Wood some
presents?

ALMA. Yes. A pair of silk pyjamas, a new suit, and then a ring
for him to give to me.

O'CONNOR. Now, it has been strongly suggested that there
was some very sinister significance in this hotel visit only a
few days before the murder. It has in fact been represented as
a kind of premature honeymoon. What truth is there in that?

ALMA. Oh, none at all. It wasn't the first time we'd gone to a
hotel, and he did love it so. He loved being waited on and
called 'sir' –

O'CONNOR. And you wanted to give him that pleasure?

ALMA. Yes.

O'CONNOR. And that was the reason for the presents?

ALMA. Yes.

O'CONNOR. And the ring to yourself?

ALMA. The ring was only a pretence.

O'CONNOR. A pretence of what?

ALMA. Well – like an engaged couple.

O'CONNOR. So this visit was no more than a whim, designed to give Wood pleasure. What about you? Did it give you pleasure too?

ALMA. No. It was terrible.

O'CONNOR. In what way terrible?

ALMA. Oh, rows.

O'CONNOR. Serious rows?

ALMA. Not on the surface. But underneath, of course, they were. You see, he knew I was trying to finish it.

O'CONNOR. Finish the relationship?

ALMA. Yes.

O'CONNOR. Why?

ALMA. Well, it had got out of hand.

O'CONNOR. Had you told him that?

ALMA. I tried to often, but the difference in our ages made it so difficult. After we'd got back from London I was determined to say 'finish for good' – and mean it. I'm quite sure he knew that, which is why he was making my life hell... I'm sorry, my lord. Dreadful...

JUDGE. Hell will do. Now, I am not sure I have followed this. You say you tried to break the affair with Wood but were unable to – one of the reasons being the difference in your ages. Surely that very thing would make it easier?

ALMA. No, my lord. Sorry, but it makes it harder.

JUDGE. But surely the older party must be the dominant party?

ALMA. Excuse me, my lord, but to me it's the other way round. Anyway, it was with me and George. I think it must be with many people. Of course, I don't know.

O'CONNOR. Now, Mrs Rattenbury –

JUDGE. One moment, please, Mr O'Connor.

The JUDGE *finishes writing then signals* O'CONNOR *to continue.*

O'CONNOR. Mrs Rattenbury. We come now to your return to the Villa Madeira two nights before the murder. Did your husband ask you any awkward question when you saw him?

ALMA. No. It was as if I'd never been gone.

JUDGE. He must surely have asked you about your operation?

ALMA. No, my lord.

O'CONNOR. Anyway, all was normal at the Villa?

ALMA. Oh yes. Very friendly.

O'CONNOR. How was Wood?

ALMA. Well, he was a bit sulky. He'd wanted to stay on at the hotel, you see. But he perked up later.

O'CONNOR. You had intercourse that night?

ALMA. Oh yes, everything normal, as you said.

O'CONNOR. Thank you. Now we come to Sunday, the day of the murder.

ALMA. Oh no. No. I can't – I…

O'CONNOR. One moment, Mrs Rattenbury, please.

ALMA. But I can't – I can't –

O'CONNOR. Please. Please.

ALMA *is silent.*

My lord, in view of the obvious difficulties which I see your lordship has noticed, I would crave your indulgence at this point to embark upon a somewhat unusual course. With your lordship's permission, I would like to quote certain passages from the signed statement entered by the prosecution yesterday, which was made by the prisoner Wood on the day of his arrest – Exhibit 27, my lord.

JUDGE. But that is evidence against Wood. You are asking to use it on Mrs Rattenbury's behalf?

O'CONNOR. Naturally, my lord. I would hardly use it against her.

CROOM-JOHNSON. My lord, I must most strenuously object to any part of the statement being read on behalf of Rattenbury. What cannot in law be used against her, must not in law be used for her. My learned friend should know that very well.

O'CONNOR. I really do not need lessons in law from prosecuting counsel. I do know that it is my duty to my client to use any evidence on her behalf that this court will allow – any evidence, of any kind, and from any source.

CROOM-JOHNSON. But, my lord, there are no precedents for such a –

JUDGE. Yes, yes, Mr Croom-Johnson. It is plainly a matter for me. You are perfectly correct in saying that this proposed course is highly irregular – but having regard for the undoubted fact that the law always allows, and must allow, the greatest possible latitude to the defence in a capital charge, I will decide in favour of Mr O'Connor.

O'CONNOR (*plainly delighted*). Thank you, my lord.

CROOM-JOHNSON *sits*.

CROOM-JOHNSON (*muttering*). ... dangerous precedent...

The lights fade to O'CONNOR *and more dimly on the* JUDGE.

I refer your lordship to paragraph three, in which –

WOOD *is heard describing the events of the murder.*

WOOD (*off*). 'They were up in her bedroom together – That is, Mr and Mrs Rattenbury, my lord.'

JUDGE. I have it, thank you, Mr O'Connor.

The light on the JUDGE *fades out.*

The light fades up on WOOD, *listening outside the bedroom door.*

O'CONNOR. 'When I went up with the tea, the door was locked. So I listened outside, and then I heard them – kissing noises and "darling". And then I heard them doing it. I listened to them right through, then I heard them talking and getting off the bed, so I went into my room and waited for them to come out…'

The lights come up on the Villa Madeira. WOOD *goes to his room. The bedroom door opens and* RATTENBURY *comes out, putting on his jacket.* ALMA *has a dressing gown on. She helps him down the stairs, which he has to take very gingerly.*

ALMA. Gently does it, Ratz. That's right… So I'll tell the Jenks we'll be over tomorrow, shall I?

RATTENBURY. If they'll have us.

WOOD *appears, a menacing figure at the top of the stairs. He is in his shirtsleeves.*

ALMA (*gaily*). Of course they'll have us. They're always asking us to stay. How long shall I say? A couple of days?

RATTENBURY. It's a long way to go for a couple of days. Lot of petrol. Make it a week.

ALMA. All right, dear.

WOOD (*calling*). Alma, I want to see you.

ALMA (*looking up*). Come down then.

WOOD (*commandingly*). Up here. Now.

RATTENBURY (*muttering*). You shouldn't let him talk to you like that, Alma.

ALMA (*shrugging*). He's in one of his moods – back in a jiffy.

She climbs the stairs. WOOD, *in a passion, grabs her wrists.*

WOOD. Why was that door locked?

ALMA. Locked? Was it?

WOOD. You lying bitch –

ALMA (*laughing*). George, you *can't* think that me and Ratz –

WOOD *opens the door and looks inside.*

WOOD. Yes. Tidied up the bed now, haven't you? You were at it just now with him, weren't you? I heard.

ALMA. Oh, George, you are a scream! Ratz, of all people. Oh, I'll die of laughing –

WOOD *hits her hard.*

(*Angry.*) George, if you ever do that again –

WOOD. You'll what?

ALMA. Tell you to get out of this house and never come back –

WOOD *produces a revolver from his pocket.*

WOOD. I could kill you quite easily.

ALMA (*calmly*). Yes, I expect you could, dear, but not with Christopher's water pistol.

She takes it from him quickly.

George, are you all right?

WOOD (*shouting*). Why was that door locked?

ALMA. Quiet, dear. Even Ratz could have heard that.

He hasn't. He is in the sitting room, placidly reading the paper.

The door was locked because it rattles when the window's open – as you should very well know. (*Strokes his face.*) Silly boy!

She gives him back the water pistol.

WOOD. Are you going to these people tomorrow?

ALMA. Yes.

WOOD. With me driving?

ALMA. Of course.

WOOD. I see. Where will I sleep?

ALMA. Oh, they've lots of room.

WOOD. In a servants' attic?

ALMA. Well, perhaps, but I'll try and see it's a nice one.

WOOD. And eat in the servants' hall?

ALMA. George, it's only for a week –

WOOD. And you and Ratz, with a nice big double bed – ?

ALMA (*angrily*). Stop this nonsense at once! At once, do you hear?

WOOD. Yes, ma'am. Very good, ma'am. Beg pardon, I'm sure, ma'am.

She turns her back on him and picks up the phone.

ALMA (*into phone*). Could you give me Bridport 31, please? This is Bournemouth 309.

WOOD (*to her, and taking the phone out of her hand*). Listen, you cow. You're to go down there now – (*Pointing to the sitting room.*) and tell him you're not going to the Jenks' tomorrow –

ALMA. George, you're going to make me very angry.

WOOD. Because if you don't, I'm going to do something very bad. Something very very bad.

ALMA. Put acid in that water pistol and squirt it in my face? (*Takes the telephone. Into phone.*) Hallo? (*To* WOOD.) Go into the kitchen and help Irene with supper, there's a good boy.

Obediently he goes, half into shadow, and then turns to listen.

(*Into phone.*) Hallo. Is that Mrs Jenks?… Alma Rattenbury… Ratz and I wondered if we could take you at your word and come over for a few days… (*To* WOOD.) Go on, ducky –

WOOD. I'm warning you, Alma. Something really *bad* –

ALMA (*into phone*). Well, I thought tomorrow, if you could have us – Oh, that *is* nice… Yes, we'll drive over… I've a chauffeur now, you know. Lovely, see you soon. Goodbye.

WOOD *runs out.*

Fade out except for the spot on O'CONNOR, *and dimly on the* JUDGE.

O'CONNOR. Wood's statement continues –

The light on the JUDGE *fades out.*

'I went to my dad's and borrowed the mallet. Then I went back. I could see them through the French windows, playing cribbage. Then she went up to bed. So I went into the room and hit him three times on the back of the head with the mallet. Then I went into the garden and hid the mallet. Then I went up to bed.'

The light on O'CONNOR *fades and comes up on the Villa Madeira. In the sitting room, very dimly seen, is the slumped figure of* RATTENBURY *in the armchair. Upstairs* ALMA *is in bed in pyjamas, reading.*

ALMA (*calling*). George!

WOOD (*off*). Yes.

ALMA. Where have you been all evening?

WOOD (*off*). Out.

ALMA. What are you doing?

WOOD (*off*). Getting undressed.

ALMA. You want to come in?

Pause.

WOOD *appears in the passage, dressed in silk pyjamas. He goes into* ALMA*'s room, and slips off his pyjamas, letting them drop on the floor.*

(*Lovingly.*) That's no way to treat three-guinea pyjamas, my lad –

He climbs into bed. She kisses him. He turns on his back.

WOOD. I'm in trouble, Alma. Real trouble.

ALMA. 'Real trouble'? There's no such thing, that's what I always say –

He turns over again, his back to her, and begins to cry.

This is a lovely world, and we're all meant to enjoy it. Now, come on. Look at me –

WOOD. I can't.

ALMA. Well, at least then tell me what it is.

WOOD. I can't… It's Ratz.

ALMA. What about him?

WOOD. I've – hurt him –

ALMA. You had a fight?

WOOD. Not a fight… I wish it had been a fight.

ALMA. Have you hurt him badly?

WOOD. Yes. Very badly.

Suddenly there is a hoarse sound from RATTENBURY, *whose head falls forward.*

ALMA (*rising*). Was that him?

WOOD. It must have been. I thought I'd killed him.

She sits up in bed.

ALMA. What have you done to him?

There is another sound from below.

(*Calling.*) I'm coming, Ratz, I'm coming, darling.

She puts on a blue kimono, lying on the end of the bed. He clutches her arm.

WOOD. Don't go down.

ALMA. I must. If he's hurt badly, I must help him –

WOOD. I've done for him, Alma. You won't get him back –

ALMA (*running down the stairs*). I'm coming, Ratz darling. I'm coming.

She runs into the darkened sitting room. After a moment she lets out a loud scream.

WOOD *gets back into his pyjamas and leans over the banisters again.*

IRENE *comes out of her room.*

IRENE (*to* WOOD). What's the matter?

WOOD. Don't know, I'm sure.

She gives him a suspicious glance, then runs down the stairs, just as ALMA *comes out of the sitting room staggering from shock.*

IRENE. What is it?

ALMA. Ratz. Someone's hurt him, Irene – Agh! Dr O'Donnell. Run out and get Dr O'Donnell. Quick, Irene – quick… Tell him Ratz may be dying.

IRENE runs out of the front door. We still don't see RATTENBURY clearly, but as ALMA approaches the chair his body suddenly slumps out of it on the floor. ALMA gives a gasp and runs away. Then she kneels at his side. WOOD has come into the room.

Ratz – my darling Ratz – help's coming soon. Stay alive, please stay alive – Ratzie, can you hear me?

WOOD has approached the body.

WOOD. It's no good, Alma. I told you upstairs I'd done for him, and I have.

ALMA. Oh no, no – he isn't dead. He can't be. Ratz… Ratz –

WOOD pours her a large whisky, and makes her drink it. It makes her retch.

Why did you do this? Why, why?

WOOD. I had to. He was stealing you away from me.

ALMA. Oh God, you little idiot. He wasn't stealing me – he couldn't have – Look, oh my God! He's –

She points to RATTENBURY's trousers, where he has fouled himself. Again ALMA retches.

WOOD. I told you I was going to do something really bad –

ALMA. To *me*. I thought you meant to *me*.

She takes off her kimono, and covers RATTENBURY *with it.*

Oh God, poor Ratz. Why didn't you kill me?

There is a ring at the front door.

Go upstairs. Go to your room. Don't come down here unless you're sent for, and then know nothing about it. Nothing at all, do you understand?

There is another ring at the front door.

Go upstairs.

WOOD *turns to go.*

WOOD. What'll you tell them?

ALMA. I'll think something up. Coming?

O'CONNOR. 'I'll think something up'... 'I'll think something up.' And what she thought up was the ludicrous mad story she told the police. Was it the story of a sane, calm, balanced woman? Or was it not a story thought up in panic by a woman in a deep state of shock, aggravated by repeated doses of whisky, and desperate at all costs to save the life of her lover?

CROOM-JOHNSON. You're addressing the jury! My lord, really I must object. Counsel is addressing the jury.

JUDGE. Yes, I quite agree. Mr O'Connor, that was highly improper. The time for your address to the jury is not yet, as you very well know. That was really highly improper.

O'CONNOR. I'm so sorry, my lord, you are, of course, quite right. I'm afraid I was momentarily carried away. I do apologise to my learned friend, and to you, my lord.

JUDGE. Have you finished with Wood's statement?

O'CONNOR. Yes, my lord.

JUDGE. And you propose to continue your examination on more conventional lines?

O'CONNOR. Indeed, my lord.

JUDGE. Then first I must address a few remarks to the jury, and try to make certain important matters clear. Ladies and gentlemen of the jury, I trust you understand that what you have just heard read to you is a statement made by the prisoner Wood, and cannot be used in any way at all as evidence against the prisoner Rattenbury. If you have heard anything you consider prejudicial to Mrs Rattenbury, you must put it completely out of your minds. I trust that is clear. Very well, Mr O'Connor, you may proceed.

O'CONNOR. Thank you, my lord. Now, Mrs Rattenbury, I'm going to ask you a very important question. Is there any part of that statement of Wood's that is in any way inaccurate or untrue?

JUDGE. Mrs Rattenbury, you must answer the question.

O'CONNOR. Is there?

ALMA *shakes her head*.

Mrs Rattenbury, is any part of that statement inaccurate or untrue in any way?

ALMA. . . . No.

O'CONNOR. None whatever?

ALMA. No.

O'CONNOR. Thank you. And what you thought up, was the ludicrous mad story that you told the police. . .

CROOM-JOHNSON. Is that a question?

O'CONNOR. It is a question. Mrs Rattenbury, have you ever in your life suffered a greater shock to your mind, body and spirit than you suffered that night when you found your husband battered to death by your lover?

CASSWELL *and* CROOM-JOHNSON *are both on their feet*.

CASSWELL *and* CROOM-JOHNSON. My lord –

O'CONNOR. – *Presumably* by your lover?

ALMA. No. Nothing ever – in all my life.

O'CONNOR. These stories of your dancing semi-nude, making advances to policemen, playing the gramophone at full blast – did they or did they not come as a complete surprise to you when they were told to you as late as three weeks ago?

ALMA. Yes, they did.

O'CONNOR. And what was your overriding emotion on hearing of them?

ALMA. Shame. Deep, deep shame.

Pause.

O'CONNOR. Mrs Rattenbury, three last questions. Did you murder your husband?

ALMA. No.

O'CONNOR. Did you take any part whatever in planning his murder?

ALMA. No.

O'CONNOR. Did you, in fact, know a thing about it until Wood told you, in bed upstairs, that he had done it?

ALMA. No. If I'd known, I'd have prevented it.

O'CONNOR. Thank you. That is all.

He sits down. ALMA *starts to leave the box.*

CROOM-JOHNSON (*getting up quickly*). Just a moment, Mrs Rattenbury, you're not finished yet. I have some questions to ask you. In fact, a great many questions.

The lights fade.

The lights come up on CROOM-JOHNSON*'s cross-examination of* ALMA*, which has now been in progress for some hours. She is very tired.*

… Mrs Rattenbury, just how old was Wood when you first invited him into the Villa Madeira as your lover?

ALMA. I didn't invite him – not in the way you mean. He insisted on living in –

CROOM-JOHNSON. '*Insisted*'?

ALMA. Why not?

CROOM-JOHNSON. But surely you could have resisted him easily, a boy of seventeen?

ALMA. Not 'easily' at all. Ever since this case began, the one thing I've heard is how I must have dominated this boy. Well, I can only say that if anyone dominated anyone else, it was George who dominated me –

CROOM-JOHNSON. Very interesting, but let us please stick to the facts. You have admitted, have you not, cheating your husband out of a considerable sum in order to take your lover up to London. Was that done under Wood's '*domination*'?

ALMA. It was his idea.

CROOM-JOHNSON. And The Royal Palace his choice of hotel?

ALMA. No. That was mine.

CROOME-JOHNSON. And whose idea was it buying the engagement ring?

ALMA. It wasn't an engagement ring.

CROOM-JOHNSON. Well, whatever it was, who suggested buying it?

Pause.

ALMA. I did.

CROOM-JOHNSON. Indeed. Now, let us return once more to the evening of the murder. This purported conversation – this alleged confession of Wood's – took place in your bedroom?

ALMA. Yes.

CROOM-JOHNSON. But I understood that your sexual meetings usually occurred in Wood's room?

ALMA. Yes. That was because of little John sleeping in mine.

CROOM-JOHNSON (*a shade wearily*). That night then little John was somewhere else?

ALMA (*almost equally weary*). No. He was in my room.

There is a murmur in court. CROOM-JOHNSON *instantly perks alive. The* JUDGE *looks up. Even* O'CONNOR *looks unhappy.*

CROOM-JOHNSON. Little John was in your room?

ALMA. Yes, but sound asleep.

CROOM-JOHNSON. Your lover climbed into your bed with your little son in the same room?

ALMA. Yes, but he was sound asleep.

CROOM-JOHNSON. Used this to happen often?

ALMA. Well, it had to sometimes, when Christopher was home.

CROOM-JOHNSON. Your lover would clamber into bed with you and you would indulge in sexual congress, with your six-year-old child in the same room?

ALMA. But he's a very sound sleeper.

CROOM-JOHNSON. A little child of no more than six summers –

O'CONNOR. My lord, I fail to see how any of this is pertinent, unless, of course, my learned friend intends to call little John as a witness in rebuttal of his mother's testimony.

CROOM-JOHNSON. I find that remark in the most appalling taste –

O'CONNOR. And I find these constant references to little John's presence in that room – a cheeild (*Pronounces it so.*) of no more than six summers – autumns, winters and springs come to that – I find these slurs on my client's moral character not only in appalling taste, but immoral, unfair, and entirely irrelevant. Who killed Francis Mawson Rattenbury? Isn't that what this court is convened to find out? It is surely not whether an act – or several acts – of sexual congress were committed in the distant presence of a heavily dormant child.

CROOM-JOHNSON. I trust my learned friend will have breath for his final address –

O'CONNOR. You need have no fear of that.

JUDGE. Gentlemen, please. This is becoming more of a cockpit than a court of law. I think Mr O'Connor is right, Mr Croom-Johnson. You have asked the witness a question – a perfectly relevant one in my view – and she has answered it. Pray let the matter rest there.

CROOM-JOHNSON. As your lordship pleases. Now, I want to be absolutely fair to you, Mrs Rattenbury –

O'CONNOR (*muttering*). 'Fair'?

CROOM-JOHNSON. When Wood, in bed with you, with your little boy in the corner –

O'CONNOR. My lord.

CROOM-JOHNSON. I have not asked my question yet.

JUDGE. Please ask it, Mr Croom-Johnson.

CROOM-JOHNSON. When Wood told you that night that he had hit your husband with a mallet, did you believe him?

ALMA (*her voice a weary croak*). Not at first. No.

CROOM-JOHNSON. When you went downstairs and found your husband had indeed been hit on the head, did you believe him then?

ALMA. Well, one naturally would, wouldn't one?

CROOM-JOHNSON. You are here to answer my questions, not to ask them of me, madam.

ALMA. I see. Well, I did believe that he had done it then.

CROOM-JOHNSON. It is my duty to submit to you that you knew Wood had done it because you had encouraged him to do it? (*After a pause.*) Well?

ALMA. I'm sorry. Was that a question?

CROOM-JOHNSON. It was a question, Mrs Rattenbury, and a very important one.

ALMA. I thought I'd answered it. Still, if you want it again. (*Raising her voice*.) I did not plot my husband's death. It was a great shock to me. I have never, in all my life, harmed a human being.

CROOM-JOHNSON. You have never 'harmed a human being'?

Pause.

ALMA (*on the edge of tears*). Not meaning to. Not till now.

The JUDGE *indicates to* CROOM-JOHNSON *to continue*.

CROOM-JOHNSON. Mrs Rattenbury, in answer to my learned friend you said that if Wood had told you of his intention to murder your husband you would have prevented it. How would you have done that?

ALMA. I'd have told him not to dare do such a wicked thing.

CROOM-JOHNSON. Would that have been enough?

ALMA. The way I'd have said it it would.

CROOM-JOHNSON. But I thought you said he dominated you?

ALMA *does not reply*.

Well – supposing you had failed to persuade him, what would you have done?

ALMA. Gone to the police, I suppose.

CROOM-JOHNSON. But after the murder, the police were all over the house. Why did you not tell them then?

ALMA. That was different.

CROOM-JOHNSON. Why?

ALMA. Well, Ratz was dead and I suppose I felt responsible.

CROOM-JOHNSON. I beg your pardon?

ALMA. I said – I suppose I felt responsible.

CROOM-JOHNSON. 'Responsible.' Thank you.

He sits down. O'CONNOR *gets to his feet, stifling a yawn – an old trick of his*.

O'CONNOR (*languidly*). Only two questions, Mrs Rattenbury – (*Straight at* CROOM-JOHNSON.) only *two*. By the word 'responsible' did you mean criminally responsible for your husband's murder?

ALMA. No.

O'CONNOR. Did you mean morally responsible for your lover's protection?

ALMA. Yes. That's exactly what I meant.

O'CONNOR. Thank you, Mrs Rattenbury. That is all. That is the case for the defence of the prisoner Rattenbury, my lord.

JUDGE. Very well. I think that is a convenient moment to adjourn...

ALMA seems momentarily entirely ignored.

The lawyers rise, stretch, and gather their papers, as the JUDGE *perfunctorily nods three times, and leaves his chair.* MONTAGU *has seen* ALMA *delaying in the box. He assumes rightly that she has not the physical strength to regain the dock – nor, perhaps, the moral strength either. He goes to the box through his preoccupied colleagues, and offers her his arm.*

MONTAGU. You did very well – very well indeed.

She seems not to have heard.

(*Comfortingly.*) Your job is done now.

ALMA (*in a hoarse whisper*). Yes.

Fade out on the court as ALMA *and the lawyers leave.*

The lights come on in MRS DAVENPORT's *sitting room.* STELLA *is on the sofa, her head deep in a newspaper.* MRS DAVENPORT *comes in.*

MRS DAVENPORT. Has Tony called yet?

STELLA. Tony? No. He hasn't. Well? How was Mrs Rattenbury?

MRS DAVENPORT stops, but doesn't reply.

My God – she must have dominated that boy. Did she –

MRS DAVENPORT *laughs harshly.*

What's so funny?

MRS DAVENPORT. Yes, I suppose that's how it must seem.

STELLA (*appalled*). 'Seem'? Edie, you're not saying –

MRS DAVENPORT. I'm not saying anything.

STELLA. Yes, you are. I know you too well. 'That's how it must seem.' Edie – she's an awful, awful woman. Sleeping with that boy with her baby in the room –

MRS DAVENPORT. What's that got to do with whether she committed murder?

STELLA. Everything, I should have thought –

MRS DAVENPORT. Then you don't know the law.

STELLA. It seems as if I don't know you.

MRS DAVENPORT. Perhaps you don't. It's that word – 'dominated'. All the time, all the time that man was on at her: 'You were twenty years older, madam. Twenty years older. I put it to you – you dominated that boy.' Do you know what she answered? 'When an older person loves a younger, it's the younger who dominates because the younger has so much more to give.'

Pause.

STELLA. And you thought of Tony?

MRS DAVENPORT. Of course.

STELLA. My God, to think that a murderess could go free just because a jurywoman overloves a son who doesn't give a damn for her.

Pause.

I'm sorry. I shouldn't have said that.

MRS DAVENPORT. You did.

STELLA. Tony rang me, this afternoon. We had a talk. A long one –

MRS DAVENPORT. In which he told you he didn't love me?

STELLA (*trying to embrace her*). Oh my God, darling. I only said that because I was so damn angry with you.

MRS DAVENPORT. Tell me what he said.

STELLA. Well, his father's got him a hundred per cent. It's a love affair.

MRS DAVENPORT. What does he want to do?

STELLA. Live with him, of course.

MRS DAVENPORT. For ever?

STELLA. Yes.

MRS DAVENPORT. Supposing I fight?

STELLA. They'll fight back.

MRS DAVENPORT. How?

STELLA. Tony will tell the Judge he prefers his father to you… Do you really want that? Of course, he said he'd spend some of his holidays with you.

MRS DAVENPORT. How kind…

STELLA. Darling, I do know how dreadful all this is for you. But you must try and forget about it, at least until this awful trial's over. Now, why don't you put your feet up, let me get you a drink. Darling, I know it's difficult for you, but you've a big responsibility tomorrow. You're not going to let this terrible business here cloud your judgement about that woman, are you?

MRS DAVENPORT. No. I'm not.

Fade out.

Before the lights come on again we hear the voice of CASSWELL.

Then a spot illuminates his face, while another focuses on ALMA's.

CASSWELL....When this boy met the woman, he was an ordinary innocent English boy, four months later, what do we find? A confessed adulterer, a confessed thief, a confessed cocaine addict, utterly under the influence of an hysterical, lying, drunken woman of abnormal sexual appetites and apparently of no moral conscience whatever...

The voice merges smoothly into CROOM-JOHNSON's.

CROOM-JOHNSON....Can you believe a single word that such a woman says – self-confessed liar, self-confessed adulteress, self-confessed seducer of a tender youth of seventeen?... A woman who, by her own admission, robs her husband of a considerable sum, in order to indulge herself in a four-day sexual orgy at the Royal Palace Hotel, with a boy young enough to be her son...

The voice is merged with that of O'CONNOR.

O'CONNOR. Ladies and gentlemen. One of your number – I cannot, of course, mention her name, which would be most improper, but I suppose I can say that she must be one of the foremost among you, a lady, evidently, of great moral courage and strength of character – she objected to serving on this case. 'Why?' asked his lordship. 'Because,' she replied, 'I am so prejudiced against Mrs Rattenbury's moral character that I cannot be expected to give her a fair trial.' But how could she not be prejudiced against this woman? How could any one of you fail to feel disgust and nausea at the ensnaring and degradation of a helpless youth by a middle-aged woman of licentious and degenerate habits? But that is not the offence with which she is charged here in this court.

The voice merges into that of the JUDGE, *speaking in a matter-of-fact tone to the jury.*

JUDGE. Well, there it is. That is the woman. It is indeed difficult to find words in the English language in which you may see fit to describe her. But, members of the jury – the natural disgust you may feel for this woman must not – I repeat that – *must not* make you any more ready to convict her of the crime of murder. In fact it should, if anything, make you *less* ready to do so. Prejudice, dislike, disapproval, disgust, must have no part in your verdict. Well, that is all I have to say to you. You will now retire…

The lights have faded to a blackout. A spot picks up the quiet white face of ALMA, *which, during the whole of the foregoing judicial onslaught on her character, has shown no sign of emotion whatever. Nor does it now as the lights come up in her cell.* JOAN *is with her.* ALMA *is sitting in a hard chair, immobile.*

JOAN. Look, dear, they may be a long time. Would you like to lie down? It'll have to be the floor – but I've had two blankets sent in, and a pillow – and I can make you quite comfy.

There is no reply from ALMA. *It is as if* JOAN *had never spoken.*

Or I've brought some cards. How about a little game?

ALMA (*at length*). Beg your pardon?

JOAN (*showing the cards*). A little game, dear. We could have much longer to wait.

ALMA. No, thank you.

JOAN. Anything at all? Coffee? Tea?

ALMA. No.

JOAN. Not with a drop of something in it?

Pause.

ALMA*'s stare continues, unseeing.*

Try not to fuss, dear. What I always tell my ladies –

MONTAGU *comes in.*

MONTAGU (*with a cheerfulness he doesn't feel*). Well, Mrs Rattenbury – how are you feeling?

ALMA *seems unconscious of his presence…*

(*To* JOAN, *in a low voice.*) Is she all right?

JOAN (*indignantly*). How could she be, after all that was said about her upstairs?

MONTAGU. I should have warned her.

He pulls a chair alongside ALMA*'s and touches her arm.*

ALMA (*quite brightly*). Oh, hullo, Mr Montagu –

MONTAGU. You must try to understand why Mr O'Connor had to say those things about you. They must have been horrible to hear –

ALMA. Not particularly.

MONTAGU. But, you see, both Mr O'Connor and the Judge, by saying all those foul things about you, *forced* the jury to concentrate their minds on only one thing – did you or did you not commit murder? Well, as we all know, you didn't –

ALMA. Do you?

MONTAGU. Of course. So does Mr O'Connor.

ALMA. And Christopher?

MONTAGU. And Christopher, most certainly.

ALMA. Then it really doesn't matter what the jury think, does it?

Pause.

MONTAGU. Mrs Rattenbury, I have every hope that in a matter of hours – or even minutes – you will walk out of this place a free woman. If you do, what plans have you made?

ALMA *says nothing.*

JOAN. Her friend Irene Riggs is taking her to her home for a few days –

MONTAGU. Oh. That's good.

JOAN. She'll be all right there – she's fond of Irene.

MONTAGU. And then you must think of taking up your career again –

ALMA. My career?

MONTAGU. As a songwriter.

ALMA. Oh, that –

JOAN (*eagerly*). Yes, dear, you must. Just imagine how your songs will sell now.

ALMA laughs harshly. MONTAGU gives JOAN a silencing look.

WARDER (*off*). Jury coming back.

ALMA. Mr Montagu, I want to thank you –

MONTAGU. Don't. You have, and always will have, my admiration.

ALMA. Oh, that's nice. That's the way men used to speak to me.

As they go out, fade into blackout. In the darkness we hear the sound of the lawyers returning to court. The CLERK OF THE COURT enters.

The lights come up on MRS DAVENPORT and dimly on the CLERK OF THE COURT.

CLERK OF THE COURT. Members of the jury, are you agreed upon your verdict?

MRS DAVENPORT. We are.

The lights come up on ALMA and WOOD, standing in the dock.

CLERK OF THE COURT. Do you find the prisoner Percy George Wood guilty or not guilty of murder?

MRS DAVENPORT. Guilty, but we should like to add a rider to that. A recommendation to mercy.

CLERK OF THE COURT. Do you find the prisoner Alma Victoria Rattenbury guilty or not guilty of murder?

MRS DAVENPORT. Not guilty.

The court hears a storm of booing, hissing and shouts of 'Shame!' – but we do not hear it. Light fades up on the JUDGE.

CLERK OF THE COURT (*hardly heard*). And those verdicts are the verdicts of you all?

MRS DAVENPORT. They are.

The storm of booing is apparently renewed. The light fades out on MRS DAVENPORT.

JUDGE. This will not be tolerated.

The storm subsides.

CLERK OF THE COURT. Percy George Wood, you stand convicted of murder: have you anything to say why the court should not pass judgement on you?

WOOD (*with a smile at* ALMA). Nothing at all.

JUDGE. Percy George Wood, the jury have convicted you of murder, with a recommendation to mercy. That recommendation will be forwarded by me to the proper quarter, where it will doubtless receive consideration.

They hear cries from the gallery of 'Don't worry, boy! We won't let them do it!', etc.

Meanwhile, my duty is to pass upon you the only sentence which the law knows for the crime of which you have been convicted.

The black triangle is placed upon the JUDGE*'s wig by the* CLERK OF THE COURT.

The sentence of the court upon you is that you be taken from this place to a lawful prison, and thence to a place of execution, and that you there be hanged by the neck until you are dead, and that your body be afterwards buried within the precincts of the prison in which you shall have been confined before your execution. And may the Lord have mercy on your soul.

The JUDGE *nods for* WOOD *to be taken down.* ALMA *fiercely grabs his arm as if she would stop him.*

WOOD. Goodbye, you silly cow.

WOOD *goes off.*

JUDGE. Let Alma Victoria Rattenbury be discharged.

The light fades out on the JUDGE.

The lights fade up on the court.

O'CONNOR *is warmly shaken by the hand by* MONTAGU, *less warmly by* CASSWELL, *not warmly at all by* CROOM-JOHNSON.

ALMA *stands meanwhile, bewildered, in the dock.*

ALMA *is approached by* IRENE, *her face wreathed in an ecstatic smile. She too embraces her.*

IRENE. I knew it! I never had a moment's doubt. Now, here you are, darling. (*Unfolds a mackintosh.*) Just slip into this. That's right. Now, we'd better have the scarf.

ALMA *takes it off obediently, to have it replaced with a simple beret.*

Now, just till we get home –

She slips on to ALMA*'s nose a large pair of horn-rimmed glasses.*

There's a policeman waiting going to show us out of a special door.

O'CONNOR (*turning*). Ah, Mrs Rattenbury. I'm so very pleased –

IRENE. Come on, dear. That policeman's waiting.

ALMA *and* IRENE *leave the court.*

O'CONNOR. Well, Croom-Johnson, may I congratulate you on an admirable performance. Of course, you had a hopeless case – but you fought it very well.

CROOM-JOHNSON. Thank you – I must warn you that I intend to raise the matter elsewhere of your directly appealing to a member of the jury by name –

O'CONNOR. 'By name'?

CROOM-JOHNSON. Forewoman?

O'CONNOR. Fore*most*, dear fellow. Fore*most*. Your hearing's letting you down.

CROOM-JOHNSON. It was, in my view, unpardonable – and I will say so.

O'CONNOR. Really! You mustn't let a little setback sour you, dear fellow. Been playing much golf lately?

CROOM-JOHNSON. Not much. Excuse me. (*Goes.*)

O'CONNOR (*gleefully*). Bad loser. I've always said so.

CASSNVELL (*approaching*). Well, O'Connor. Magnificent. The boldness of it staggered me.

O'CONNOR (*chuckling*). Yes. I took a risk or two.

CASWELL. There was a moment when I actually thought you were pleading with the jury to have the woman burned as a witch.

IRENE *has appeared, breathless.*

IRENE. Mr O'Connor – she's disappeared – Alma's disappeared –

O'CONNOR (*his mind elsewhere*). Alma?

IRENE. She suddenly ran right across the street and disappeared –

MONTAGU. What happened?

IRENE. Just now. There was this bus, I thought she was going under it. I shouted to her – but she didn't seem to hear. She just ran and ran.

MONTAGU. She knows your address. She's probably going there.

IRENE. But she doesn't.

MONTAGU. Well, the best thing to do is to go back to where she left you. She's bound to come back when there's no one else around –

IRENE. No one recognised her, I'm sure. Shouldn't I tell the police?

MONTAGU. There's not much they can do. I'll come with you.

They exit.

O'CONNOR. Really, women of that class do panic so easily.

The lights come up on MRS DAVENPORT*'s flat.* STELLA*'s standing belligerently facing the door through which* MRS DAVENPORT *has just entered.*

STELLA. Well? What happened? Edie?

MRS DAVENPORT has gone straight to the drink tray, and poured herself out a large whisky.

MRS DAVENPORT. Didn't you hear it on the news?

STELLA. Come on, Edith. I've only got a few minutes. I mean, how did you let it happen? What was the voting?

MRS DAVENPORT. Let's think… I was at the head of the table, which is where they put the Forewoman.

STELLA. What's the matter with you? Are you drunk?

MRS DAVENPORT. Yes, I am a bit. (*Takes a long swig.*) Well, each person spoke up, and I took the votes down. That was my job, you see.

STELLA. The voting. How was the voting?

MRS DAVENPORT (*suddenly brisk*). Five for guilty, and six for not.

She replenishes her drink.

STELLA. So your vote made it six all.

MRS DAVENPORT. No. My vote made it seven-five. Then all the others gave way.

STELLA. Gave way to you?

MRS DAVENPORT. Yes.

STELLA. In God's name, why?

MRS DAVENPORT. Because she was innocent.

STELLA. Innocent?

MRS DAVENPORT. Of murder.

STELLA. Innocent! Who was it who said that nothing was too bad for that woman, that she deserved lynching?

MRS DAVENPORT. She may deserve that. She does *not* deserve hanging for a murder she didn't commit.

STELLA. What does that matter, for God's sake?

MRS DAVENPORT. It matters to me.

STELLA. Well, what price your pretty little house in Bournemouth now.

MRS DAVENPORT. But – but no one in Bournemouth knows that I was on the –

STELLA. Oh, of course they did.

MRS DAVENPORT. I see. Well, I'll have to stay on in this flat.

STELLA. Looks like it.

MRS DAVENPORT. And I hate it.

STELLA. I know. I must go – (*At the door*.) Poor Saint Edith, what's to become of you?

She goes out. The lights on the flat partially fade, as MRS DAVENPORT *pours herself a large neat whisky and then slowly sits.*

Meanwhile, ALMA *stumbles to centre stage. She sits, and at length she gets a pencil and a few crumpled envelopes from her pocket.*

She starts to write.

The lights come up on a little man, the CORONER, *sitting at an insignificant desk. He reads quietly from a folder in front of him.*

CORONER. Coroner's report in the matter of Alma Rattenbury deceased. William Mayfield, labourer, of this parish of Christchurch, stated that at about 8.30 p.m. on June fourth he was walking across a meadow through which ran a stream. On the bank of the stream he saw a lady sitting and writing. He crossed the stream by a bridge and went down the bank the other side. As he did so, he looked towards her and saw the lady standing, a knife in her hand. He ran back towards her but before he could reach her she had stabbed herself in the body five or six times, three of the wounds penetrating the heart. When he reached her she was dead, her head lying in one foot of water... I do not propose to read all the documents found beside the body. Mostly they appear to be random thoughts scribbled in pencil on the backs of envelopes and suchlike – but here is one. It begins: 'I want to make it perfectly clear that no one is responsible for my action. I made up my mind during the trial that if George was sentenced to death I would not survive him – '

He looks up at an unseen court.

In this context I might mention as an unhappy chance that had Mrs Rattenbury lived only a few more days she would have heard of the reprieve accorded to George Wood by the Home Secretary.

He turns to his folder.

Now, here are what must be her very last words as the paper was found under her body with the pencil still on it.

ALMA. Eight o'clock. After so much running and walking I have got here. I should find myself just at this spot, where George and I once made love. It is beautiful here. What a lovely world we are in, if only we would let ourselves see it. It must be easier to be hanged than to have to do the job oneself. But that's just my bad luck. Pray God nothing stops me. God bless my children and look after them. One has to be bold to do this thing. But it is beautiful here, and I am alone. Thank God for peace at last.

MRS DAVENPORT *gets up unsteadily, carrying her whisky. We now see she is really very drunk.*

MRS DAVENPORT (*suddenly shouting*). But I gave you life! I gave you life!...

She sips her drink, shaking her head.

(*In her most Kensington voice*.) And, might I say, at some considerable cost to my own?… Really, there's no justice…

She laughs and drinks. ALMA *takes out* CHRISTOPHER*'s Scout knife. As she looks at it, the lights fade out.*

The End.